LITERARY LIBATIONS

WHAT TO
DRINK WITH
WHAT YOU READ

AMIRA MAKANSI

ILLUSTRATIONS BY
ELENA
MAKANSI

Skyhorse Publishing

Skyhorse Publishing books may be purchased in bulk at special discounts for sales promotion, corporate gifts, fund-raising, or educational purposes. Special editions can also be created to specifications. For details, contact the Special Sales Department, Skyhorse Publishing, 307 West 36th Street, 11th Floor, New York, NY 10018 or info@skyhorsepublishing.com.

Skyhorse® and Skyhorse Publishing® are registered trademarks of Skyhorse Publishing, Inc.®, a Delaware corporation.

Visit our website at www.skyhorsepublishing.com.

10 9 8 7 6 5 4 3 2

Library of Congress Cataloging-in-Publication Data

Names: Makansi, Amira, author.
Title: Literary libations : what to drink with what you read / Amira Makansi
    ; illustrations by Elena Makansi.
Description: New York : Skyhorse Publishing, [2018]
Identifiers: LCCN 2018017880| ISBN 9781510736580 (hardcover : alk. paper) |
    ISBN 9781510736610 (Ebook)
Subjects: LCSH: Cocktails. | Drinking of alcoholic beverages. | Drinking of
    alcoholic beverages in literature. | Popular literature--Bibliography. |
    LCGFT: Cookbooks.
Classification: LCC TX951 .M24 2018 | DDC 641.87/4--dc23 LC record available at
https://lccn.loc.gov/2018017880

Cover design by Jenny Zemanek
Cover illustration by Elena Makansi
Interior design by Christine Schultz

Print ISBN: 978-1-5107-3658-0
Ebook ISBN: 978-1-5107-3661-0

Printed in China

CONTENTS

INTRODUCTION

WHY BOOKS AND BOOZE?

If you're at a bookstore looking at this book, odds are you're a person who loves to read, or at least likes to read, or maybe you're pretending you like to read to impress your love interest, or to convince your parents you're not wasting your twenties living in their basement (yes, Mom, I am doing something with my life—reading the entire Western canon counts as "something," right?). Or maybe you just picked up *Infinite Jest* or *Underworld* and you're already trembling a little from the sheer effort of *lifting* the damn thing, by now wondering why on earth this bookstore doesn't sell beer. Perhaps you finally picked up your copy of *Fifty Shades of Grey* (because you're lying to yourself if you "don't want to read it") and are dying for a taste of Christian Grey's luxurious lifestyle but have no idea where to start beyond handcuffs and hot wax. Or maybe, like me, you suffer from chronic reading anxiety about the fact that this bookstore is really freakin' big and there's literally no way you will ever be able to read every book under this roof, even if you wanted to, and are in dire need of an alcoholic beverage or some smelling salts to calm your nerves.

Well, you've come to the right place. Whether impressing a crush, tackling a stupidly long tome like *Infinite Jest* or *Ulysses*, or chronically anxious about the vast quantity of reading material in the world, this little text offers the solution to all your literary problems. The answer is booze. Whether drowning your sorrows after a tearjerker like Markus Zusak's *The Book Thief* or self-medicating your way through Cormac McCarthy's *The Road*, this book offers drink pairing recommendations for more than 150 classic and contemporary novels to get you through the best of times, the worst of times, and the most boring of times. I'm looking at you, Jonathan Franzen. (Just kidding. I haven't even read your books yet.)

Maybe you've gotten this far into the introduction and you're about to put the book down because you're reading along and thinking, *But what's the point, Amira? Why do I need to know what drink goes best with my favorite book? Why can't I just pour myself a shot of vodka and be done with it?* That, my friend, is the million-dollar question. And the answer is:

Because books—and booze—are so much more complicated than that. Because a great novel and a great drink both have the power to transport you. Because our memories are stronger when coupled with aromatic experiences.* And because a story shared between friends is always better over a pint of beer.

Reading and drinking are both about empathy and connection. Reading allows us to empathize with the characters. Sharing a drink signals that we are in trustworthy company and opens us up to connecting with others. Both involve sharing in another person's experience or culture. Both allow us to deepen connections, experience new things, and relax and enjoy ourselves.

---

*This is scientifically true. Memory formation is positively influenced by experiences in taste or smell. In other words, if you smell something strong in a particular moment, you're more likely to remember it. Why do you think people love pumpkin spice and autumn leaves? Because they're powerful and pleasant sensory experiences.

Every pairing in this book has been carefully researched to ensure that the book and the drink are tied together, at least loosely, by some historical or thematic thread. It doesn't make much sense to pair a whiskey drink with a Russian novel, does it? Nor does it make sense to drink champagne with a work of Shakespeare—as delightful as it might be to sip bubbly while reading *Much Ado About Nothing*, champagne literally hadn't been invented when Shakespeare was writing.

For the sake of convenience, the chapters are organized by genre. Love sci-fi? There's a whole category for you. Prefer your novels esoteric and intellectually elitist? Skip to contemporary literary fiction. Are you under the age of twenty-one? Don't worry, I've got suggestions for you, too. Hop, skip, or jump to the children's and young adult pages, where I've got nonalcoholic pairings for every book listed—with a few boozy suggestions tacked on, because we all know these books aren't just for kids.

ON LITERARY GENRES AND CLASSIFICATIONS

All books have been ordered chronologically by publication date within their assigned genres. If you have a complaint about the way I've categorized the books, or which section a particular book was shelved under, I've got two words for you: stuff it. In the introduction to Constance Barrett's translation of *War and Peace*, A. N. Wilson simultaneously quotes and criticizes of one Tolstoy's early reviewers: "'It is neither a novel nor a novella,' wrote one fool, as though it matters what category you put a book into." I couldn't agree more. By and large, I don't believe that books should be categorized at all, as great books of any kind transcend genre. If you have a problem with any of these categorizations, I advise you to take your pompous literary taxonomy elsewhere.

If, however, you merely wish to understand rather than to judge my system of categorization, with the underlying assumption that great novels straddle and encompass multiple genres, I will say this: my guiding light was whatever the predominant narrative or theme is in the book. Some might wonder why Emily Brontë's *Wuthering Heights* is included in the European Classics section, while her sister Charlotte's *Jane Eyre* is found in the Romance section. This is because Jane's relationship with Edward Rochester forms the backbone of Charlotte's tale, while Heathcliff's romance with Catherine is short-lived, tempestuous, and serves more to explain how Heathcliff became such a miserable character than to inspire any romantic sentiment. Similarly, *Fahrenheit 451* by Ray Bradbury is less a science fiction novel (the science doesn't play a large role, and books could be burned as easily in Bradbury's time in as his invented future) than a book about authoritarianism; by contrast, *Frankenstein* not only uses science fiction as an analogy for hubris but also relies on science fiction for the backbone of the plot.

And if you're wondering why your favorite novel hasn't been included in this volume, then you must go up to the cash register and buy ten copies of this book *immediately*, so my publisher will commission many more editions and I can advise you what to drink with all your favorite books—sadly omitted in this edition, but certain to be included in forthcoming volumes—and we can all live happily ever after.

A NOTE ABOUT THE PAIRINGS

If I had simply gone through every book and paired it with the drink most often mentioned in the pages, half these books would be paired with shots of whiskey, half with some variation on a martini, and half with Tokaj. (Yes, that's too many halves. See? Impossible.) That would have been a witless way to pair drinks with books and would have made for incomparably dull reading. We're aiming to capture the spirit of the book, not to replicate the drinks within the pages, which is why these pairings are by no means restricted to the drinks mentioned in the book. In many cases, the pairings are region- and period-specific, by which I mean the drink recommendation would have been available in the book's time and place. In some cases, though, I made exceptions, opting for pairings based more on taste, theme, and spirit than historical or geographical relevance.

It's no secret that some of my favorite books have been paired with some of my favorite drinks. A whiskey sour was my gateway into cocktails; it's been paired with my favorite book, *Catch-22*. (The drink's components match so perfectly with the book's themes. Can you blame me?) When I'm reaching for something nonalcoholic, ginger beer is my go-to, which is convenient because it so perfectly captures the spirit of Lyra Silvertongue, the charismatic heroine of Philip Pullman's *The Golden Compass*, my favorite book as a child.

Some of the books I've chosen are from authors with dozens of internationally successful books—in these cases, I shamelessly chose to write pairings for the books I've read, seen the film adaptation, or (in the worst of cases) actually heard of. Don't judge me. I had to pare down this list *somehow*. Did I mention chronic reading anxiety yet? This bookstore is really big. Especially if you're at Powell's. They don't call that place a "city of books" for nothing.

A FEW MORE NOTES ABOUT THE PAIRINGS . . .

These pairings are nothing more than recommendations. Suggestions. Ideas. Random thoughts. Hazardous guesses. ("Hazarded"? "Haphazard"? I must head to Dictionopolis for the correct word posthaste.) The best pairing for any book is whatever gets you in the mood to read. You don't like my pairing? Get creative. According to the laws of mathematics, there are countably infinite ways to combine the many various alcoholic and nonalcoholic beverages in a single glass. At least a few of those have to taste good. Get inventive. Seek out new flavors. Definitely *do* try this at home. (But don't sue me if something goes wrong.)

Next, a few things about selecting your drinks.

By and large, I have tried to provide general recommendations for the books contained herein. This is because distribution laws vary by state, and some brands or producers might be available in one area but not in another. It doesn't make sense to recommend a specific Burgundian wine producer when that producer is only available in three states. Nor does it make sense to recommend an obscure brewery or distillery when they only have regional distribution. This is not to say you should not support your local distillers and masters of fermentation. You should. In the interests of national book buyers supporting local producers, I have left these pairings general, so you can find examples within the style that are locally available and work with your palate.

LEARNING AND UNDERSTANDING WINE

Buying wine can be nearly as scary as buying books, particularly if you're just beginning to learn about wine. Wine labels—with their diverse regions, varieties, producers, and labeling regulations—can be an enormous challenge to interpret and understand. Sometimes, when starting out, it's reasonable to feel as though wine producers are trying to trick you, by leaving information off their labels or expecting you to have a basic knowledge of wine geography in order to interpret the labels. In nearly every case, it's best to defer to an expert. Try not to buy wine from a grocery store. With a few exceptions at premium grocery stores (my adopted state of Oregon's Market of Choice is one), there will be no one there with any knowledge worth acquiring. Find a wineshop within reasonable distance and make friends with the staff. Ask them what's new in the store, what they're enjoying, and what they're drinking at home. Ask why some bottles are long and skinny, while others are short and stocky. Ask how to pronounce "Crémant de Bourgogne" so you don't sound like a fool when you buy a bottle to impress your date. Wine suffers from far too much pretension, and the best way to break that stigma is to ask questions and learn from the experts.

THE DEMOCRACY OF BEER

These days, beer is a much more democratic pastime than wine. Far more people know things about beer than know things about wine. This is partly because beer is cheap. But it's also because beers are generally better at telling you what the thing inside the bottle will taste like. Generally, if it's a pilsner-style beer, that is, a medium-bodied pale lager with Czech hops, it says "pilsner" somewhere on the bottle. (Wine producers could learn a thing or two from this kind of straightforward, elegant system.) This doesn't mean it's possible to become an expert in beer overnight. You'll need to drink a lot of the stuff—woe is me!—talk to the experts, ask questions, and seek out new experiences. Over time, you'll find your favorite breweries and styles, and you'll be able to confidently pick out a Belgian *framboise* even if you think *framboise* is pronounced like the capital of Idaho. (It's not.)

COCKTAILS AT HOME AND AT LARGE

The world of cocktails is fast and loose and changing every day. It is my professional recommendation that you drink heavily to learn as much about them as possible. Experiment with many different brands of spirits to find which ones you like best: which are best on their own, which work well in cocktails, and how they all play together. There are a few basic rules of thumb to remember when making cocktails at home or ordering them at a bar. Here they are, in no particular order.

- If a cocktail calls for citrus juice, always use fresh-squeezed. Do not fool yourself into thinking you can substitute that acid water in the lemon-shaped bottle that's been sitting in your fridge for a year and a half. The only exception to this is a mimosa, where you can use bottled orange or grapefruit juice without too much reduction in quality.

- Same goes for herbs. Dried mint—dried anything—is never a substitute for fresh.

- Garnishes are always optional but always preferable to a naked cocktail (unless no garnish is specified).

- Cocktails are malleable, but it's better to be precise on your proportions. The liquor-sugar-acid balance is a fine line and upsetting it will result in an unpleasantly tart or candy-sweet drink. It's better to switch lime for lemon if you're running low than to use ½ ounce lemon juice when a recipe calls for a full ounce.

- Many cocktails call for some quantity of simple syrup. I always have simple syrup on hand at home, as it is quite easy to make. Simply mix 1 part water and 1 part sugar in a small saucepan (I like to do 1 cup each) and heat until the sugar is completely dissolved. Do not boil. Simple syrup will keep for a week or two on the counter, or several weeks in the refrigerator. After a certain point, it may crystallize. You can either warm it again to bring the sugar back into solution or throw it out and make a new batch.

- Experiment. Taste everything you make. Try again. Mixology is as much a skill as an art form, and you will get better with practice.

DARK AND STORMY
THE CLASSICS, EUROPEAN EDITION

Hold on to your hat, and get ready to get boozy. Depending on your perspective, these long-standing classics are either intense, emotional reading experiences or fantastically boring. These recommendations are liquor-heavy cocktails or robust beers and wines, designed to get you drunk enough to think the author really was a genius, after all.

The Odyssey

HOMER

Pairing: Greek Red Wine

I can hear your thoughts. *Duh. What else would you drink with Homer? But which one, Amira? There are so many to choose from!* Not necessarily. If you live in New York, sure—you can almost certainly get your hands on a lovely bottle of dark red wine from the Ionian island chain, to which Odysseus's beloved Ithaka belongs. But if you live in a small town in Missouri, it might be well-nigh impossible. Perhaps the best way to help you find the right wine pairing is to outline a simple set of criteria with which to choose a bottle. Here are the rules you should follow: (1) Both the wine and the grape variety should be Greek in origin (for example, Syrah and cabernet sauvignon are not welcome here); (2) it should not be fortified, as distillation was still four thousand years away when Homer's epic took place, and; (3) it should be red. Although white wine is serviceable, you won't get the same experience. After all, he sang of the "wine-dark sea," not the "wine-light" sea.

Hamlet

WILLIAM SHAKESPEARE

Pairing: Mulled Wine

Set in the frigid Kingdom of Denmark and laden with enough existential angst to torture even a Buddhist monk, you'll need something to warm your soul through this dark and potent story. Mulled wine is simple enough to make and will provide you with enough alcohol to trudge through the bitter depths of this play while reassuring you that there really is a light at the end of the tunnel. Break a leg, and remember to check your glass for poisoned pearls before you tip your cup.

INGREDIENTS (SERVES 6–8)
½ cup brown sugar
20 cardamom pods, approx.
3–4 sticks of cinnamon
1 tablespoon whole cloves
1 teaspoon crystallized ginger
2 bottles (750 mL) red table wine
2 cups white port wine
Raisins, for garnish
Slivered almonds, for garnish

INSTRUCTIONS

1. In a large mixing bowl, combine brown sugar, cardamom, cinnamon, cloves, and ginger with red wine and white port.

2. Allow this mixture to sit for at least 1–2 hours, but ideally overnight.

3. Before serving, heat the mixture on the stove in a nonaluminum pan and bring to a gentle simmer. Do not allow the mixture to boil (or you will cook off all your alcohol, and what a waste that would be!).

4. When the mixture is heated through and the spices well-incorporated, strain through a sieve.

5. Garnish with a handful of raisins and slivered almonds.

6. Serve hot.

The Ingenious Gentleman, Don, Quixote of La Mancha,

MIGUEL DE CERVANTES SAAVEDRA

PAIRING: BRANDY DE JEREZ SOLERA

Although temptation might lead you to pair this delightfully mad comedy with the rum brand named after the title character, this would be a mistake. Rum had not yet been invented, let alone brought to Europe, when Cervantes published his comedic novel about the ridiculous adventures of Don Quixote. But brandy, a spirit distilled from wine grapes, was not only available but growing in popularity at the time. Airén, the most commonly grown grape variety in Castilla–La Mancha, has long been a critical ingredient in Spanish brandy, which brings us to the home province of our rollicking adventurer. Not to mention that the packaging on a fine bottle of Spanish brandy is as almost as flashy and absurd as Quixote himself. Pour yourself a glass of Brandy de Jerez (neat, in a snifter) and allow this chivalrous spirit to carry you through the hills and towns of old Spain.

Gulliver's Travels

JONATHAN SWIFT

Pairing: Navy Grog

While pondering the origins of the words "Brobdingnagian" and "Lilliputian" and wondering how Gulliver's adventures managed to go so awry, you'll want to sip something that represents the seafaring Age of Discovery. Rum, a spirit derived from fermented, distilled sugarcane or its derivatives, was created in the Caribbean during the colonizing years of sugar plantations, and thereafter was a mainstay on ships both commercial and military. Representing as it does the naval and commercial dominance of the British, rum neatly summarizes the phrase, "the sun never sets on the British Empire." For centuries, rum was rationed out to sailors to keep morale up and infections at bay. But grog—the real thing—is a drink I wouldn't wish on anyone. Watered-down rum straight out of the barrel is not my idea of a good time. Fortunately, an enterprising bartender whose name might have been Donn Beach invented a much more enjoyable tiki cocktail called Navy Grog at a Hollywood establishment in the '30s. This drink is similar to the real thing in spirit, but unlike grog, it actually tastes good. Citrusy, fruity, and spritzy, a Navy Grog cocktail will keep you bubbly as you giggle your way through Swift's satirical parody of contemporary travelogues.

Note: To make this cocktail, you'll need to make a different kind of simple syrup with honey first. Fortunately, this is very easy to make and requires not more than a half hour's forethought, so long as you have honey on hand.

INGREDIENTS

½ cup honey

¼ cup warm water

1 ounce Demerara rum

1 ounce dark rum (Jamaican, such as Gosling's)

1 ounce light rum (Cuban or Puerto Rican, such as Bacardi or Havana Club)

¾ ounce lime juice

¾ ounce grapefruit juice

¾ ounce club soda

Orange slice, for garnish

Cherry (fresh or maraschino) for garnish

INSTRUCTIONS

1. First, make the honey syrup. Combine the honey and warm water in a bowl and stir well to mix. Set aside to cool, if you have an hour or more before making the cocktail. Or place in the refrigerator, but be careful not to leave for too long, or the honey may crystallize.

2. When the syrup has reached room temperature, combine 1 ounce honey syrup with all other ingredients (except soda water and garnishes) in a cocktail shaker.

3. Fill shaker with ice, shake well, and strain into a Collins glass filled with ice.

4. Top with soda and add the orange slice and cherry.

Candide

VOLTAIRE

Pairing: Volnay

"I serve your Beaune to my friends, but your Volnay I keep for myself,"
Voltaire is rumored to have written to his friend, famous négociant Louis
Latour. Volnay is a specific AOC (Appellation d'Origine Contrôlé) within
the Burgundy region, renowned worldwide for the pinot noirs and chardonnays grown and produced there. The vineyards from Volnay produce
a pinot noir light in structure but rich in clarity and finesse, reflecting a
delightfully optimistic view on life while retaining the earthy character
that makes Burgundy one of the best-loved wine regions in the world.
Like the poor, naïve Candide, you will believe Pangloss's preachings that
"all is for the best," as this fine, light wine carries you through the best of
all possible worlds, through the fires of Lisbon and the ravages of war,
through the Incan jungles and into the utopian El Dorado. The rocky,
mineral structure of this wine will lead you back to the earth alongside
Candide and his new bride as they settle down to cultivate their garden.

The Count of Monte Cristo

ALEXANDRE DUMAS

PAIRING: BANYULS, VIN DOUX NATUREL

Could anything but strong, evocative fortified wine match the mystery and intelligence represented by the Count of Monte Cristo? Fortified wines are popular around the world but were historically more popular when dry wines were not always of such good quality as they are today. Port is the most famous fortified wine, but there are many different types produced around the world. In France they are called *vin doux naturel*, and Banyuls, an AOC in the Languedoc-Roussillon, is one such region where these wines are produced. Banyuls sits at the northern border with Spanish Catalonia, which is where the opening scene of Dumas's brooding tale of riches and revenge takes place. Banyuls, often made from the elegant Grenache variety and fortified with brandy, is as strong and charismatic as Edmond Dantes, and as enigmatic and potent as the Count of Monte Cristo. Just don't try to finish the book—or the bottle—in one night.

Wuthering Heights

EMILY BRONTË

PAIRING: BRANDY HOT TODDY

"Proud people breed sad sorrows for themselves," Mrs. Nelly Dean says to Heathcliff, neatly summing up the entirety of *Wuthering Heights*. But if you insist on reading it despite that I've just told you the whole story, and in spite of Brontë's savage characters and their bitter passions, I've got just the thing to get you through. A strong hot toddy will warm you through this coldhearted tale and calm your nerves as the characters torment each other. Brandy, drunk occasionally in Brontë's "wild, confused, disjointed, and improbable" novel, was a popular drink in England with all social classes, where cognac in particular gained favor with the aristocracy via enterprising London merchants in the seventeenth century. (Don't waste good cognac in a hot toddy, though!) Hot tea mixed with some strong spirit would doubtless have been served to Mr. Lockwood during his convalescence, and we ought to share one with him while we listen to Mrs. Dean's cruel and tragic story.

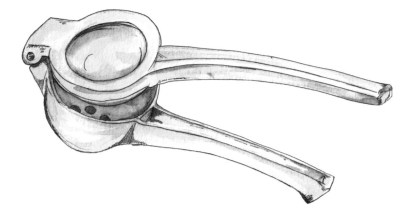

INGREDIENTS

6 ounces hot water

1½ tablespoons honey

1 tea bag (black tea preferred, such as English Breakfast, Earl Grey, or Darjeeling), or, if using loose-leaf, 1 teaball full of leaves

¾ ounce fresh lemon juice

2 ounces brandy (V.S. or V.S.O.P. recommended—nothing fancy needed for this drink!)

Cinnamon stick, for garnish

INSTRUCTIONS

1. Bring the water to a boil. While you are doing so, coat the bottom of your serving mug with the honey.

2. Pour hot water over the honey and stir to dissolve the honey. Add the tea bag (or ball) and let steep for 3–5 minutes.

3. Remove the tea bag and mix in the lemon juice and brandy. Garnish with the cinnamon stick and serve hot.

Madame Bovary

GUSTAVE FLAUBERT

PAIRING: CALVADOS, PAYS D'AUGE

As Emma Bovary grows wilder and wilder with her romantic and financial excesses, plumb the depths of your own bank account with this fine apple brandy from the region of Flaubert's birth, the Pays d'Auge. Calvados, an excellent brandy distilled from apple cider (and occasionally a small portion of pears as well) is a dry but fruity liquor from the northwestern region of Normandy. The finest of these sumptuous brandies come from the Pays d'Auge, which is conveniently very near the small towns that provide the backdrop for Emma's affairs. Best enjoyed in a brandy snifter, aged Calvados will transport you to the place and time of Flaubert's famous novel, and, if you drink enough, will send you into a spiral of madness right alongside the adulterous and indulgent Madame Bovary.

A Tale of Two Cities

CHARLES DICKENS

PAIRING: BORDEAUX

What better to drink with this classic tale about the overthrow of the aristocracy than a bottle of the wine that best represents the aristocracy? With the French Bordeaux houses (called chateaux, or castles) ruling the world of wine, and some bottles running upward of ten thousand dollars apiece, this is an excellent beverage to drink in order to fully appreciate why the French wanted to overthrow the aristocracy in the first place. Known as "claret" to their English counterparts, these world-renowned wines would have been enjoyed by the aristocratic Charles Darnay and his English counterpart Sydney Carton alike. But fear not, friends—not all Bordeaux wines are so expensive. A tasteful wineshop should be able to point you in the right direction. Immerse yourself in the world of revolutionary France with this classic wine and you will find yourself carried away, as much by the emotion of the book as by the elegance and complexity of good Bordeaux.

Les Miserables

VICTOR HUGO

PAIRING: CRU BEAJOULAIS

Do you hear the people sing? You'll be singing for sure after a bottle of these delightful wines.

Fitting that this book comes chronologically right after *A Tale of Two Cities*, as both books focus on the ramifications of different French Revolutions, particularly with regards to economic class and social status. If *A Tale of Two Cities* is about the overthrow of the aristocracy, *Les Miserables* is about the desperation of the poor in the face of a changing economic structure. Cru Beaujolais wines, eloquent and expressive red wines made from gamay noir (a grape rapidly growing in popularity stateside), have much in common with pinot noirs, but are considered to be the bastard cousin of their more extravagant relatives. What better to swig while cheering for our heroic students as they set up barricades in the streets of Paris than an underappreciated symbol of the bourgeoise? Beaujolais wines from the AOCs of Fleurie, Julienas, and Saint-Amour are some of my personal favorites.

War and Peace

LEO TOLSTOY

Pairing: Imperial Russian Stout

Vodka on its own, for all that it captures everything we think of as Russian, is too straightforward for this tale of Homeric proportions. Tolstoy's epic, which spans thirteen years, has arguably influenced the course of Russian history and has been called "the best novel that had ever been written," cannot so easily be distilled down. We need something with depth, complexity, and length on the palate. We need something that hits many different flavor components and encompasses the broad swath of the human experience, from Napoleon the infamous conqueror to Karataev the forgotten peasant. Enter the Imperial Stout, a style that emerged in the late eighteenth century when czarina Catherine the Great commissioned barrels of strong English beer for Russian consumption. Royal in both name and character, with a broad range of flavors, a rich and wide mouthfeel, and a strong dose of alcohol, these beers make the perfect accompaniment to Tolstoy's riveting tale of clashing empires.

Heart of Darkness

JOSEPH CONRAD

PAIRING: PETITE SIRAH

Petite Sirah has the dark heart to match Conrad's *Heart of Darkness*. Inky black in color and with rich, round, opulent flavors, this wine will carry you deep into the Congo, through the brutal history of colonialism, and into a slow but steady descent into madness. This wine will pair equally well with existential discussions of race, identity, and insanity. Some stunning Petite Sirahs are being made in California right now, particularly from the Paso Robles area, or from Sonoma and Mendocino in the north. These wines are so dark and so serious, you may want small portions of rich food to balance them out. To deepen your pairing, open a second bottle and put on *Apocalypse Now*, the 1979 reinterpretation of the story set in Vietnam. Sit back and wait for the film—and the wine—to blow your mind.

The Brothers Karamazov

FYODOR DOSTOYEVSKY

PAIRING: TOKAJI ASZU

There's something about these rich, complex narratives and characters that draws me to dessert wines. Maybe it's the layer upon layer of flavor. Maybe it's the addition of sweetness as a textural component. Maybe it's the velveteen texture, the succulent palate shape, the way the finest dessert wines make me think of the ambrosia drunk by the gods of Olympus. *The Brothers Karamazov* is the literary version of that ambrosia, so divinely layered and lush that even while describing violence and depravity, Dostoyevsky sounds like he's singing a Homeric poem. Tokaji Aszu, hailing from Hungary, is sweet like the Sauternes of Bordeaux or the *eisweins* of Germany. The sweetness is rich and uplifting like brother Aloysha, while the intricate flavors of this kingly wine represent the layers and depth of Mitya and Ivan. Sip as slowly as you read. Savor every flavor and every word. You'll find as much depth in both book and drink as you care to seek.

The Picture of Dorian Gray

OSCAR WILDE

PAIRING: BRANDY AND SODA

Brandy for the bloodred stain on Dorian Gray's beautiful hands; soda for the hedonistic life and eternal youth for which he sacrifices his soul. Get high-quality brandy—not one of the finer cognacs or Armagnacs, which should be reserved for a snifter, but a step above well-grade—for our vain and wealthy antihero, and simple, unflavored soda water. (None of that grapefruit La Croix here. I'm looking at you, millennials.) It was a popular drink at the time in England, as it was easy to make at home and allowed the drinker to enjoy a lighter, more refreshing incarnation of brandy, an enduring British favorite. This drink has the added advantage of actually being featured in the book: Basil Hallworth, the painter behind the portrait of the young Dorian Gray's inimitable beauty, enjoys one of these in his fateful final encounter with the titular character. Make this cocktail as pretty as you like, but please don't sell your soul for its sake.

Note: This cocktail, and the entire "Liquor and Soda" category of cocktails, should be made to taste. Make it as strong or as bubbly as you like. Dorian supports your choice to make it a double.

The Metamorphosis

FRANZ KAFKA

PAIRING: ABSINTHE

Only something as psychologically stimulating as absinthe—the real stuff, not the watered-down version we get in America—can get you in the right mind-set to appreciate Kafka's bizarre tale of transformation, guilt, and disgust. Absinthe, first distilled from wormwood, fennel, and anise in Switzerland, spread like wildfire among the poets and artists of Europe in the nineteenth century. By 1915—the year Kafka's most famous work was published—it was outlawed in nearly every European nation, thought to be dangerously psychoactive and addictive. (We clearly had no idea what would hit us with the introduction of LSD in the 1950s.) In recent decades it has seen a revival, and this vibrant spirit is potent enough to convince you that you, too, might wake up mysteriously transformed into a giant bug one day.

(continued on page 20)

A note on drinking absinthe: there is an extensive history and ritual behind the consumption of absinthe. To enjoy this drink properly, according to the tradition known as "la louche," *follow these steps:*

1. Prepare your drinking glass—it should be clear, not opaque, so you can watch the absinthe transform from clear to opalescent—by setting it on a saucer and setting a perforated spoon or knife over the glass. The spoon is traditional, but a knife more easily straddles the glass.

2. Set a sugar cube on the perforated knife.

3. Pour one ounce of absinthe over the sugar. This will start the process of dissolving the sugar into the drink.

4. Slowly drip or pour ice-cold filtered or purified water over the sugar cube, continuing the dissolution process. Depending on how strong you want your absinthe, you will want between three and five parts water for every part of absinthe.

5. When you are finished pouring out the water, if there is any sugar left on the knife, stir it into the glass and serve.

Ulysses
JAMES JOYCE

PAIRING: IRISH WHISKEY, NEAT

With *The Odyssey* we drink the essence of Greece (page 2); with *Ulysses* we'll drink the essence of Ireland. In truth, no drink could capture the totality of Joyce's magnum opus. It's too wild, too various, too all-encompassing to find a single drink that would fit for every page. Here, we'll have to settle for second-best. But contrary to the popular idiom, second place isn't always last place, especially where good whiskey is concerned. It may take one a stiff one or two to get you drunk enough to pretend to understand *Ulysses*, unless you're an academic, in which case the pretending probably comes a little easier. Either way, straightforward Irish whiskey is the only drink that will both set the scene in Dublin on June 16 and lubricate your brain cells enough to digest the enormity of this novel. Keep it simple, keep it neat, and remember that no matter how liquid your consciousness gets, it won't come close to what's on these pages.

Mrs. Dalloway

VIRGINIA WOOLF

Pairing: Amontillado Sherry

Sherry gets a bad rap in modern drinking culture, not unlike books written by women about women which dare to claim equality with books written by men about men. Virginia Woolf's most famous novel is a brief but powerful meditation on memory, language, psychology, and the nonlinear nature of time. Amontillado sherry reflects the nuanced process of aging and the complexities of flavor and character. These fortified wines from the D.O. of Jerez in Spanish Andalucía go through a unique, extended transformation to emerge in this distinct style. The base wine is made from the Palomino grape, fermented to dryness like a standard table wine, and then fortified with grape spirit to between 14.5–16 percent alcohol. What distinguishes sherry from other kinds of fermented grape products is the flor, a thick layer of benevolent yeasts that metabolize sugars into a variety of compounds, resulting in a different range of flavors and textures than are found in dry table wine. Amontillado is distinguished from fino sherry by the longevity of this yeast layer: when the flor is allowed to die, and the sherry goes through an oxidative aging period over several more years, taking on yet more flavor characteristics and deepening in color, that is amontillado. Amontillado sherry is a special, underrated beverage, and deserves its time in the limelight—just like Mrs. Dalloway. Find a good bottle and chill it before serving—it should be served about as cold as white wine. After all, as Woolf writes in *A Room of One's Own*, "One cannot think well, love well, sleep well, if one has not dined well."

Lolita,

VLADIMIR NABOKOV

PAIRING: MOSCOW MULE

It would be impossible to get through this book without a vodka pairing for a Russian author, and this pairing is near-perfect. The vodka works for the Russian origins of this dark yet whimsical story, while the spritzy ginger beer represents the innocence and excitement of childhood, and therefore, of the girl Lolita. And the fact that this high-octane drink will knock you sideways before you can say "Humbert Humbert" five times fast is appropriate, given how quickly the protagonist is knocked sideways by Lolita's youthful beauty.

INGREDIENTS
2 ounces Russian vodka
½ ounce lime juice
4 ounces ginger beer
Lime wedge, for garnish

INSTRUCTIONS
1. In a copper mug or a Collins glass, combine vodka and lime juice.

2. Top with ginger beer, a generous portion of ice, and stir well.

3. Gently squeeze a lime wedge over the top and drop it in the mixture to garnish.

NAPA CAB, KENTUCKY BOURBON, AND A MANHATTAN
THE CLASSICS, AMERICAN EDITION

Ranging in style from lighthearted and humorous to heavy and tragic, classic American literature can be broadly characterized as darkly comedic stories that don't take themselves too seriously. (At least not when compared to our European counterparts.) The drinks chosen here are all either American-made or conceived of in America, because how could a French wine represent the American zeitgeist? Our great nation can be credited to some degree with the invention of cocktails, and certainly credited with taking them to the next level during the Prohibition era, when liquors were notoriously low-quality and needed to be masked with a balanced blend of sugar and acid. But that's not all we're known for. In the last seventy-five years, America has emerged from a zero-tolerance policy on alcohol to produce some of the finest wines in the world and oversee the revolution in craft beer. I'd say that deserves a toast.

Moby-Dick

HERMAN MELVILLE

PAIRING: NAPA VALLEY CABERNET SAUVIGNON

From his bibliographic curations on the whale to his limitless allusions to famous works of literature to Ahab's thirst for domination over the forces of nature, it's clear that Melville thought himself a genius and had no qualms waving around his little flag. Whether he was or wasn't is for the reader to decide. In either case, such an ambitious book deserves an ambitious drink. This is where Napa Cab comes in. A more royal drink I can't imagine. When you endeavor to conquer the mountain that is the white whale, it's best to have something equally daring, intimidating, and powerful at hand. The only American wine to match this breadth and power is Napa cabernet, so find a bottle or several and let these two masterpieces lead you into a strange new world.

The Adventures of Huckleberry Finn

MARK TWAIN

PAIRING: WHISKEY FIZZ

To judge by this book alone, you'd be forgiven for thinking Mark Twain was a warrior for the temperance movement. Through his alcoholic father, Huck Finn notices early on that alcohol is both corrosive to men's souls and a harbinger of bad luck: just about every time one of the characters gets drunk, something bad happens to him or those around him. But the author himself enjoyed drinking occasionally, particularly with his friends, and sought to preserve his right to do so. Whiskey in particular is mentioned often enough in this novel that one can assume if Twain knew we were devising drink pairings for his book, he'd point us to the whiskey barrel. By drinking ours with bitters, lemon juice, and soda water, we can have the best of both worlds—a hydrating, revitalizing cocktail for the temperance folk and enough whiskey for those who enjoy drinking in moderation. Sip slowly and merrily as you jump aboard the raft with Jim and Huck, and enjoy Twain's scathing social commentary as you float gently down the Mississippi toward freedom.

INGREDIENTS

2 ounces whiskey
1 ounce lemon juice
½ ounce simple syrup
4–6 ounces chilled club soda
Lemon wedge, for garnish

INSTRUCTIONS

1. Combine whiskey, lemon juice, and simple syrup in a cocktail shaker. Shake well over ice for 10–15 seconds.

2. Fill a highball glass with ice and strain the cocktail into the class.

3. Top with club soda and squeeze the lemon wedge over the top. Stir gently and drop the lemon wedge into the glass.

The Great Gatsby

F. SCOTT FITZGERALD

PAIRING: FRENCH 75

A boozy cocktail with bubbles and a lemon twist served in a champagne glass? Does anything else say Daisy Buchanan quite so clearly? Not only does this charming cocktail fit the life and times of Jay Gatsby's object of obsession, it also represents the attitude of the Roaring Twenties: "Eat, drink, and be merry, for tomorrow we die." Delicate and herbal, a French 75 will keep you partying right alongside Gatsby, Daisy, Nick, and Jordan, while the liquor-heavy pours will tug you back ceaselessly into the past.

INGREDIENTS
1 ounce gin or mid-level cognac
½ ounce lemon juice
½ ounce simple syrup
2 ounces champagne
Lemon peel, for garnish

INSTRUCTIONS
1. In a cocktail shaker, combine gin or cognac, lemon juice, and simple syrup. Shake over ice for 10–15 seconds.

2. Strain into a champagne flute or a chilled coupe and top with the champagne. Twist the lemon over the top to express the oil, and drop it in.

The Sound and the Fury

WILLIAM FAULKNER

PAIRING: OLD-FASHIONED

If Faulkner's entire body of work cannot be summed up in totality by an Old Fashioned, I'll have to read his entire body of work to find out what could. The Old-Fashioned, originally known simply as a "whiskey cocktail," is one of the oldest cocktails around—pretty obvious if you take the name at face value. But it's also a drink that represents all things Southern: sweet bourbon, Christian values, the old boys' club. Legend has it that this incarnation—made with bourbon, Angostura, and a bit of sugar—was invented at a gentlemen's club in Louisville, Kentucky. This cocktail, eminently adaptable to modernity but still wistfully nostalgic, is emblematic of Faulkner's introspective novel. Through the Compsons, he simultaneously looks to the past for a purer time, criticizes the injustices of the present, and hopes for a better future in the hands of a new generation. With an Old Fashioned in hand, you can do the same.

INGREDIENTS:
4 ounces simple syrup
1 thin slice of orange
4 dashes Angostura bitters
2½ ounces whiskey
Lemon twist, for garnish
Maraschino cherry, for garnish

INSTRUCTIONS:
1. Muddle simple syrup, orange slice, and bitters together in an Old Fashioned glass.

2. Fill the glass with ice (big cubes of ice are best, to avoid dilution), add whiskey on top, and stir for 10–15 seconds.

3. Garnish with the cherry and lemon twist.

The Grapes of Wrath

JOHN STEINBECK

PAIRING: CALIFORNIA OLD VINE ZINFANDEL

Although the American wine industry was devastated by fifteen years of Prohibition, and wines of American origin were few and far between when Steinbeck's famous novel was published, the title of the book almost begs for a wine pairing. While cabernet sauvignon might reign supreme among California vineyard plantings and is probably the most celebrated variety to come out of the state, cabernet sauvignon is the aristocracy of California wine. Zinfandel is a wine for the people. Fruit-forward and jammy, light in body but rich in texture, occasionally with notes of spice, earth, and dust, Zinfandel embodies the complex and variegated terroir of California. What better to drink while reading about the working-class struggles of Depression-era Americans than an affordable wine that hails from the setting of Steinbeck's classic novel?

Their Eyes Were Watching God

ZORA NEALE HURSTON

Pairing: Citrus Shandy (Radler)

You'll want something cool and refreshing to drink as you sit on the porch with Janie Crawford and Pheoby Watson in early twentieth-century Florida. As Janie Crawford tells the story of her life in the Jim Crow South, Hurston's language is enticing like a cold beer on a hot summer's day, her story as fresh as an orange from the orchard. You'll want something unassuming and unpretentious, evocative of small-town living from a different time, but with that thirst-quenching joy that comes only when reading—or drinking—something so satisfying. Shandys and radlers are basically identical; both words mean the same thing. You'll want something representative of Florida, so look for a shandy with primarily orange or lemon. Find a brand you like and sip your way through a few bottles as you let Janie tell you the story of her life.

Gone with the Wind

MARGARET MITCHELL

PAIRING: WHISKEY SMASH

Bourbon and mint are two Southern essentials, brought together in the classic cocktail known as the whiskey smash. The name is reminiscent of Scarlett O'Hara: confrontational but engaging, charming but conflicted. A whiskey smash sweeps you off your feet like Ashley Wilkes but mocks you like Rhett Butler. It shows you the brutalities of war while reveling in the delights of the South. A smash is an iteration of a julep, another essential Southern drink, but since these particular Southerners so love their bourbon, a smash is more appropriate. A smash is a category of cocktails open to interpretation—they generally involve mint, oftentimes crushed or shaved ice (though not necessarily), have a base of spirits, and are served with fresh fruit. Although the rules are fast and loose, our Whiskey Smash will follow the classic outlines and will use peaches in honor of Mitchell's picturesque Georgia.

INGREDIENTS

¼ tablespoon (a little less than a teaspoon) sugar

1 ounce water

3–4 sprigs of mint, plus extra for garnish

3–4 thin slices of fresh peaches

2 ounces whiskey

INSTRUCTIONS

1. In an Old Fashioned glass or a steel julep cup, muddle sugar, water, and mint together.

2. Top with ice and fresh peaches, reserving 1 slice for garnish

3. Add whiskey and stir well to mix. Top with the last peach slice and a sprig of mint and serve.

For Whom the Bell Tolls

ERNEST HEMINGWAY

PAIRING: RIBERA DEL DUERO

Although most remember Hemingway as a cocktail aficionado, the author was a connoisseur of many kinds of alcoholic beverages. (He was, in fact, an alcoholic.) Wine, shared between the fictional Robert Jordan (and the actual Ernest Hemingway) and his compatriots in the Spanish Civil War, was loved by Hemingway as much as by the Spanish themselves. These serious but lively Tempranillos from the Ribera del Duero—a D.O. that encompasses Segovia, where Jordan is tasked with blowing up a bridge for the Republicans—have proved to be some of the most revolutionary European wines of the last twenty years. A region formerly known for low-quality, low-cost grapes has transformed itself into a region known for high-quality, low-cost grapes, which works out for the benefit of everyone. Polishing off a bottle of your own will give you the courage to go to battle with the fascists as well.

The Catcher in the Rye

J. D. SALINGER

PAIRING: MANHATTAN

Had Holden Caulfield had a clue what he was doing, he would have ordered a Manhattan to impress his female dancing partners. Since he didn't, we'll do it for him. The Manhattan cocktail is an American classic, made only with rye whiskey and a blend of sweet and dry vermouth. It's as New York as they come. But Holden wouldn't have liked this drink, a classy, traditional cocktail that represents the privileged wealth of New York City. "A product of the goddamn phonies," I can practically hear him saying. But Holden was the true phony, envious from a distance of the wealth and arrogance around him, critical of the lifestyle only because it rejected him. Mix yourself a Manhattan as you navigate the dark, unapologetic corners of New York City and Holden's mind.

INGREDIENTS

2 ounces rye whiskey
½ ounce sweet vermouth
½ ounce dry vermouth
2 dashes Angostura or orange bitters
Lemon twist or maraschino cherry, for garnish.
(If you prefer your drinks slightly sweeter, use the cherry. If you prefer them slightly more bitter or acidic, go for the twist.)

INSTRUCTIONS

1. Mix all ingredients except garnish in a cocktail shaker, top with ice, and stir for 10-15 seconds.

2. Strain into a chilled cocktail glass.

3. Garnish with lemon twist or maraschino cherry.

Invisible Man,

RALPH ELLISON

PAIRING: MINT JULEP

In the broad history of black Americans, there are so many individuals who have been relegated to invisibility by the forces of white supremacy, and in the more specific history of cocktail-making there are a good many African American bartenders who have been similarly maligned. From Cato Alexander, inn- and barkeeper whose tavern, Cato's, was a New York City institution for thirty-odd years, to Tom Bullock, bartender at the elite St. Louis Country Club institution and first African American to write a book on cocktails (*The Ideal Bartender*), to John Dabney, who was born a slave but bought his own freedom prior to Emancipation, these brave and defiant men (and a few women) have, by and large, been relegated to the dustbin of history. All these bartenders have one thing in common: they were famous for their Juleps. Mint Juleps were incredibly popular at the time, and a bartender could make or break his reputation by how good his Juleps were. So, fix yourself a Julep, read up on the influence of African American bartenders on American mixology and hospitality, and help make these incomparable figures from our collective history a little less invisible.

INGREDIENTS
Fresh mint leaves
½ ounce simple syrup
2 ounces whiskey or bourbon

INSTRUCTIONS
1. In an Old Fashioned glass (or in a stainless-steel Julep cup), muddle together plenty of fresh mint leaves and the simple syrup.

2. Top the glass with ice and pour over the whiskey.

Fahrenheit 451

RAY BRADBURY

PAIRING: FLAMING B-52 SHOT

It would have been improper to recommend anything but a flaming cocktail with Bradbury's cautionary tale about censorship and burning books, and a flaming B-52 fits our needs perfectly, with coffee liqueur to keep book-lovers everywhere happy and a name that evokes the bombers flying Guy Montag's dystopian city at the story's end. Be careful when you light your shot on fire—or, better yet, take your book to a bar and let the professionals do it for you. I'd prefer the book-burning scenes remain firmly in the *fiction* category, thank you.

INGREDIENTS
½ ounce Kahlúa
½ ounce Bailey's Irish Cream
½ ounce Grand Marnier (substitute Cointreau if necessary)

INSTRUCTIONS:

1. Pour Kahlúa into a shot glass.

2. Pour Bailey's Irish Cream on top to float.

3. Pour Grand Marnier (sub Cointreau if necessary) on top of the previous two ingredients to float.

4. (Optional, and possibly dangerous—use caution) To light the shot on fire, either:

   a) Use room-temperature Grand Marnier, or;

   b) Build your shot slightly shorter than normal by using less Grand Marnier than you would to fill the glass to the top. Carefully add 3–4 drops—no more—of high-proof (151 proof) rum on top of the previous ingredients.

   c) Light the shot on fire. Wait until the fire has gone out to take the shot. (I don't feel it should be necessary to clarify this last bit, but my lawyer informed me that I should.)

On the Road

JACK KEROUAC

PAIRING: ANCHOR STEAM BEER

Can't make it to the Vesuvio Café in San Francisco to drink whiskey with Kerouac's ghost? That does present a conundrum: how do you choose the perfect beverage to sip or shoot with this absurdity of a book? When everything American and intoxicating is available to us—the whole great damn country, the gamut of drugs and alcohol, the wide swath of anything that would get you high or low or upside down is consumed, worshipped, and tossed aside within these pages—how do you pare down your options? There seems to be no wrong answer, no drink or drug that doesn't fit, no substance that would not suffice to carry you through the highs and lows alongside Sal and Dean and Carlos and Marylou and Old Bull and all the rest. But when I think carefully, I realize there's something simple and straightforward in all this madness. It's Kerouac's love of "the purity of the road." The perfect pairing will capture that purity. It'll be something clear, bright, and promising. Light but enticing. You'd as soon drink it in your backyard as you would in a dark bar. You'd take it out on the road* as soon as you'd order it at a jazz club. It'll sing to you the promise of the utopian Golden State, the eternal here and now, the experience of "what is really America's most excited city." With these criteria in mind, it now seems self-evident that the single best thing to drink alongside Kerouac's master-piece is a classic American ale brewed in his dreamlike vision of Frisco. As one of America's oldest breweries, and arguably the oldest craft brewery, Anchor Steam plays a key role in American beer culture. The brewery might not be mentioned by name in *On the Road*, but Kerouac and friends drank so much beer that one can only assume they shared a pint or many while cavorting across the city. So: open a bottle of this American icon and revel in Sal and Dean's frenetic dance across the highways of America.

---

*What I meant to say was: you absolutely, definitely, positively would *never* take an open bottle of beer with you on the road. Right? Right. That's definitely what I meant.

To Kill a Mockingbird

HARPER LEE

Pairing: Muscadine Wine

If you're a fan of books, and also of cocktails, you may have noticed a book floating around called *Tequila Mockingbird: Cocktails with a Literary Twist* by Tim Federle. And while the titular drink would make an excellent pairing for this book, it would have been too easy to recommend Federle's creation as a pairing for Harper Lee's bildungsroman. Instead, sip a cool glass of Muscadine wine, an Alabama specialty, as Scout, Jem, and Dill play games, tell tales, and make mayhem in Maycomb, Alabama.

In order to understand Muscadine wine, we need to back up and explore the history of grape-growing in America. The vast majority of wines produced in America are made from *vitis vinifera*, a grapevine that was brought over from Europe with the colonizers. Most of the varieties grown commercially for wine production—pinot noir, chardonnay, or cabernet sauvignon, to name a few—are different clones of *vinifera* that were both accidentally and intentionally curated in Europe over hundreds of years. But America has its own native grape varieties, including Muscadine, which is made from vitis rotundifolia. In Alabama, it is both wild and cultivated for wine—one Alabaman I know told me Muscadine wine "reminds her of childhood."

Because the vine produces grapes naturally lower in sugar, Muscadine is often fortified with sugar before fermentation and fermented to semi-sweetness. This yields a fruity, viscous wine reminiscent of honeysuckle and ripe Concord grapes. Nostalgic and innocent, a chilled glass of Muscadine wine is the perfect drink to set the scene for growing up in small-town Alabama.

Catch-22

JOSEPH HELLER

PAIRING: WHISKEY SOUR

This cocktail hits all the pressure points: creamy, a touch of sweetness, zingy acid, and a lot of booze. With a bit of imagination, the ingredients all connect thematically with plot points from the book. An egg white for Milo Minderbinder's ability to purchase eggs for three cents, sell them for two, and still make a profit. American whiskey for Yossarian's endless desire to be grounded and come home. Italian lemons for Luciana, Yossarian's beautiful part-time girlfriend from Rome. Shaken over ice until the whites form soft peaks, like poor Dunbar's mountain. Strained into a sidecar glass—fitting for the bombardier who can only ride sidecar while the pilot and deranged navigator fly the plane. A whiskey sour or two will leave you contemplating your own sanity while Yossarian and his friends fly grimly to freedom. "Oh well, what the hell," Dunbar says. I couldn't agree more.

INGREDIENTS
2 ounces whiskey
1 ounce lemon juice
1 ounce simple syrup
1 egg white
Maraschino cherry, for garnish

INSTRUCTIONS
1. Combine whiskey, lemon juice, simple syrup, and egg white in a cocktail shaker. Top with ice and shake well, 15–20 seconds.

2. Strain into a chilled sidecar glass. Garnish with the cherry.

The Bell Jar

SYLVIA PLATH

PAIRING: AMERICAN VODKA

One might be forgiven for thinking that vodka drinks should be exclusively paired with Russian or Eastern European books, but we would be hard-pressed to find a better book to pair with vodka than *The Bell Jar*. Vodka is the only alcohol Plath's semiautobiographical character Esther Greenwood really enjoys, despite sampling many other drinks throughout the book. Vodka is intended to be neutral in flavor and is distilled and filtered multiple times to achieve purity, representative of Esther's search for purity in the world around her. American vodkas do an excellent job of achieving this neutral flavor, in contrast to European vodkas, which tend to have subtle but more definite flavor characteristics—convenient, since we're on the hunt for an American drink. Esther likes the drink because it makes her feel "powerful and godlike." (No, she doesn't want it with soda, gin, ice, or anything like that. "Just plain," she says.) What she doesn't know is that the last place in the world to seek clarity is at the bottom of a glass of vodka.

Slaughterhouse-Five

KURT VONNEGUT

PAIRING: DEATH IN THE AFTERNOON

Ernest Hemingway invented this drink, but I doubt very much if he would mind Vonnegut borrowing it. This mind-bending absinthe cocktail is the perfect thing to prepare you for Billy Pilgrim's jumps through time and space; not to mention the drink's name captures Vonnegut's serious-but-casual approach to death. "So it goes," he writes on nearly every page, his version of *requiescat in pace*, as various secondary and tertiary characters die with a frequency unmatched by any other book I've read. The cocktail's intense aromatics bring to mind one of the author's most evocative phrases, when he describes his whiskey-soaked breath as the smell of "roses and mustard gas." (I promise the cocktail is far more pleasant, and definitely not toxic.) The Death in the Afternoon cocktail matches both the grim fervor of this tale and Vonnegut's easygoing, black humor. Both will make you laugh in the face of man's darkest moments.

INGREDIENTS
1½ ounces absinthe
4–5 ounces Champagne

INSTRUCTIONS
1. Pour the absinthe into a chilled champagne flute or cocktail glass.
2. Slowly add the Champagne until the drink turns milky and opalescent.

Beloved

TONI MORRISON

PAIRING: CHAMOMILE TEA COCKTAIL

It might seem odd to pair a cocktail with a book so viscerally about slavery and its ramifications. The history of alcohol reaches its long, spindly fingers deep into the history of slavery and oppression, from the use of slave labor on sugar plantations for rum production to the practice of trading alcohol to Native Americans to encourage addiction. But *Beloved* is about uncovering repressed memories and learning, not hiding, from brutal truths. Chamomile, mentioned several times in the book as an herb that grows wild and has the power to float old memories to the surface, gives this drink its character; bourbon, Kentucky's great claim to fame, sets us where we need to be. Drink this sweet concoction and let the savory floral aromas set the stage, from Sweet Home in Kentucky to 124 Bluestone Road in Ohio, for digging up dark truths and recovering from deep wounds.

INGREDIENTS
8 ounces water
1 chamomile tea bag (or 1 tablespoon dried chamomile flowers)
1 ounce Kentucky bourbon
1 ounce simple syrup
½ ounce lemon juice
Lemon peel, for garnish
Chamomile flowers, for garnish (optional)

INSTRUCTIONS
1. Bring the water to a boil, then steep the tea for up to 5 minutes. You'll want to use a vessel you can easily pour from to steep the tea.

2. In a heat-proof glass, combine bourbon, simple syrup, and lemon juice.

3. Once steeped, slowly pour into the bourbon mix; stir to incorporate.

4. Twist the lemon peel over the top and drop in the glass. Garnish with chamomile flowers, if using.

A Confederacy of Dunces

JOHN KENNEDY TOOLE

PAIRING: BUDWEISER

A quintessentially American product for this quintessentially American work of literature. And what but a watery, off-yellow can of Budweiser pairs as well with one of Ignatius's beloved hot dogs? For John Kennedy Toole's sake, eat at least one NOLA-style hot dog (top it with hot sauce and/or chili) with a can of Bud in hand while you're reading this book. Not only is this pairing comedic enough to match the self-righteous comedy embodied by Toole's infamous protagonist, it will also get you thinking about all the things that are wrong with America (mass-produced beer tops my list), lamenting our great nation's demise right alongside Ignatius J. Reilly.

PLOT TWIST, LEMON TWIST
MYSTERY, THRILLERS, AND SUSPENSE

Many cocktails seem to have been named with thrillers in mind. From the Inside Job to the Last Word to the Death in the Afternoon, it's almost impossible not to associate these names with novels that set you on edge. But cocktails with deadly names aren't the only drinks that pair well with these haunting stories. In this chapter, you'll learn what to drink with some of the most popular books from the world's best-loved genre. You'll want to leave a light on when you go to bed—and not just so you don't trip over the cat while you stumble to the bathroom.

Crime and Punishment

FYODOR DOSTOYEVSKY

PAIRING: RUSSIAN VODKA

Unlike the more highbrow *The Brothers Karamazov*, which calls for a noble, philosophical drink, Dostoyevsky's gritty, cerebral mystery novel demands a gritty, cerebral pairing. Although it's hard to call *Crime and Punishment* a murder mystery (to quote the translator's introduction, "the most mystified character in it is the murderer himself"), it still deserves inclusion in the Mystery, Thriller, and Suspense category, as all three words apply in spades. Mystery? Check—if you consider the mystery of the human condition. Thriller? Check—never have I been so thrilled as when racing through Raskolnikov's bewildering trains of thought. Suspense? Check— so much that at times I set the book down, afraid of what I would find in the next sentence, let alone the next chapter. Of all the iconic Russian books by iconic Russian authors, the one I would most easily pour a glass of straight Russian vodka—chilled, no ice, no garnish—is *Crime and Punishment*.

A Study in Scarlet

Sir Arthur Conan Doyle

Pairing: Whiskey and Soda

Sherlock Holmes, undoubtedly the Western world's most famous detective, is aided and abetted by alcohol throughout his adventures. From gleaning clues based on the length of a wine cork to guessing at a culprit's identity by his drink preferences, alcohol and its role in society factors into Holmes's deductions throughout Conan Doyle's body of work. Nor was Holmes above partaking in mind-altering substances himself. Holmes's standby (cocaine and morphine aside) was a whiskey and soda, a simple but classic drink. It fits the times, too. Soda water was growing in popularity during the nineteenth century, as industrial techniques brought carbonation to the mainstream, but cocktails had not yet taken hold as firmly in England as across the pond. Simple mixed drinks, such as a scotch and soda or brandy and Benedictine, were common in England. Perhaps, by partaking of Holmes's favorite drink, a little of his brilliance will rub off on the rest of us.

And, Then, There Were None

AGATHA CHRISTIE

PAIRING: FINO SHERRY

This literary game of Clue holds you at arms' length from every character, rendering them all just beyond the bounds of sympathy. None seem honest, even less upstanding, so it's of little concern when the title's promise kicks in. We watch almost with pleasure as they begin to fall like the boys in *Lord of the Flies* (see page 157). Sherry, though produced in Spain, is beloved by the English of all social classes, and fino sherry is both accessible to servants and secretaries and highbrow enough for judges and generals. Sherry of any kind, at least in modern perception, has an air of superiority about it, so it's just the sort of thing you'll want to drink, eyes twinkling with malice, while you sit quietly in the corner of the room and judge Christie's deliciously unsavory characters. Sip out of an old crystal glass with your pinky crooked, and watch in delight and terror as one by one the characters mysteriously meet their ends . . .

The Big Sleep
RAYMOND CHANDLER

PAIRING: THE GIMLET

"Hard-boiled" is how many describe the works of Raymond Chandler, but his prose is as florid as a garden in Santa Monica. The tension between wealth and crime, privilege and class, style and substance, are on display in the prose, and though Philip Marlowe may be the epitome of what we now think of as the stereotypical P.I., at the time he was revolutionary. A man of manners, poise, and hard edges, Marlowe demands a classy drink. Although in this book he opts for a double scotch, that doesn't do Chandler's femmes fatales—the wild, unpredictable Sternwood girls—justice. Although *The Long Goodbye* came later, he drank a gimlet in that book. Classy is as classy does, so we'll follow his example with this high-caliber drink, which is as suited to wood-paneled smoking rooms as it is to Los Angeles courtyards.

INGREDIENTS
4 ounces vodka
½ ounce lime juice
½ ounce Rose's lime juice
Thin lime wedge, for garnish

INSTRUCTIONS
1. Combine all ingredients in a cocktail shaker over ice and shake well to mix.

2. Strain into a chilled coupe or martini glass and drop the lime slice gently over the top.

Casino Royale

IAN FLEMING

PAIRING: THE VESPER

If "shaken, not stirred" isn't one of the top five most iconic lines in movie history, I'll eat Oddjob's hat. The martini was a classic long before Fleming began writing, but the release of *Casino Royale* heralded the drink's launch into perpetual fame and glory—though no one knew it yet. It took eight years and Sean Connery to complete the process with the 1962 release of *Dr. No.* In *Casino Royale*, Fleming specifies Bond's preferences for the martini. This version is known as the Vesper, after the only girl Bond really loved. And while some gin aficionados consider any vodka martini to be an indecent betrayal of the classic, doesn't that make this pairing—and its name—all the more apt?

INGREDIENTS

3 ounces Gordon's gin
1 ounce vodka
½ ounce Lillet Blanc
Lemon peel, for garnish

INSTRUCTIONS

1. Combine gin, vodka, and Lillet Blanc in a cocktail shaker and top with ice. Shake well and strain into a chilled martini glass or coupe.

2. Twist the lemon peel over the liquid and drop it in.

The Talented Mr. Ripley

PATRICIA HIGHSMITH

PAIRING: CARPANO ANTICA FORMULA

Antica Formula vermouth—smooth and charismatic but brooding—so embodies the character of Tom Ripley it's a wonder the two weren't invented by the same person. Carpano originated in Turin in 1786 when herbalist Antonio Benedetto Carpano created what was, at the time, a formulation for health: fortified muscatel with a secret combination of vitalizing herbs and spices. Now, Antica Formula is produced with a blend of Italian white grapes as well as an herbal formulation that takes months to prepare. The result is a stunner. With sweet flavors and earthy, floral aromas, this drink is a magical cocktail ingredient but also woefully underappreciated on its own. It makes a wonderful aperitif: in the winter it's perfect on the rocks; in the summer, a splash of soda will turn it into a cooling, refreshing afternoon drink. Tom Ripley's suave but malevolent character, as well as the warm, southern Italian backdrop for this psychological thriller, go hand in hand with Carpano Antica Formula.

The Spy Who Came in from the Cold

JOHN LE CARRE

Pairing: Gin and Tonic with English gin

John le Carré is such a prolific author it's almost impossible to pick a single book to represent his body of work. Most are famous, and several have been adapted for the screen, including this one. In my quest to highlight an author's works I sometimes feel there is no better way to represent an author than via his early work, which is why I've chosen *The Spy Who Came in From the Cold* for le Carré. It's one of his darkest and one of his best. (It's also the only one I've read.) His prose is as British as it comes; if you're an American, you can't help but read in a British accent. It begs for a British pairing. We're looking for something as cold and uncaring as Cold War espionage. As hostile as the Berlin Wall. As bitter as a gunshot in the night. Gin presents itself readily as an option. A few fingers of gin, a splash of tonic water, a fresh lime, and a handful of crushed ice and you're good to go. As you drink, remember: in this world of paper-pushing spies, there are no good guys. There are only survivors.

In Cold Blood,

TRUMAN CAPOTE

PAIRING: PILSNER

In a pioneering work of investigative journalism that reads better than most novels, Capote spins names, dates, and actions into a remarkably empathetic narrative that makes you feel, like any good novel should, like you are at the scene of the crime. Like you are both victim and perpetrator. Well, I don't know about you, but after I've murdered an innocent family *In Cold Blood* and made off with a disappointing amount of cash, I'm always thirsty for a cold beer. In Kansas during the time this book is set, our only readily available option would have been a 3.2—a low-alcohol brew—which doesn't sound like quite the thing to ease the blood-on-my-hands shivers. Fortunately for us, we live in the era of the beer renaissance, and it is now possible to get a thirst-quenching and delicious beer to calm one's mind. Enter the pilsner. A beer made in the image of the American working class. Cold and relaxing enough to still your shaking hands, whether tired from a long day of farm work or restless after murdering a family of four. And, best of all, delicious. Drink up. You'll need it.

The Shining

STEPHEN KING

PAIRING: BOILERMAKER

If you've read the book, you'll understand the pairing. If you've just seen the movie, maybe you won't, but you can at least understand the need to consume as much alcohol in as short a time period as possible to understand Jack's alcoholic, demented spirit. Parts of this book, most notably Jack's recovery from alcoholism, were based on King's personal experiences with addiction. The Boilermaker, a shooter with a remarkably apropos name which involves dropping a shot of whiskey into a pint of beer, accomplishes that goal. It will warm you through the cold winds of a Colorado snowstorm, but it will coax you into deepening madness. It will make you wonder if your house is talking to you, too. And if you're lucky, it won't blow up in your face. Don't drink more than two, lest you find yourself charging through your house with a roque mallet. *Redrum*!

INGREDIENTS
1 whiskey shot
1 pint of beer

INSTRUCTIONS
1. You can either drop the shot glass into the beer and drink as a depth charge (truly, this is the way to commune with Jack Torrance's demented mind); or you can take the shot and chase it with the beer.

The Key to Rebecca

KEN FOLLETT

PAIRING: DAIQUIRI

Cairo during the Second World War was a jumbled mishmash of international cultures, from the imperialist, urbanizing force of the British to the camels and shepherds of the Bedouins. The Islamic rejection of alcohol rubbed shoulders awkwardly with the foreigners' demand for the luxuries they were accustomed to, such as cognac and champagne. All the while, Cairo experienced massive growth, gaining a reputation as an international center of commerce. Soon it wasn't just the Europeans clamoring for fancy drinks. But cognac and champagne are foreign drinks; a daiquiri can be made with ingredients all found within Egypt's borders. Sugarcane is a cash crop in Egypt, grown south of Cairo on the banks of the Nile. Indeed, one of the few spirits produced in Egypt today is rum. Add a little simple syrup and some lime juice and you've got yourself a cooling, cosmopolitan cocktail, classy enough to be served at the soldiers' bars but representative of Egyptian production. Follett's vivid descriptions of the heat of the city, the omnipresent sand, the crush of the souks, and the sweet relief of a cold drink will make you happy to have a daiquiri in hand as you race against the clock to find *The Key to Rebecca* before General Rommel gets the keys to Cairo.

INGREDIENTS
2 ounces white rum
1 ounce lime juice
1/2 ounce simple syrup
Lime wedge, for garnish

INSTRUCTIONS
1. Combine rum, lime juice, and simple syrup in a cocktail shaker. Top with ice and shake well, 10-15 seconds.

2. Strain into a chilled cocktail glass and garnish with the lime wedge.

Red Dragon

THOMAS HARRIS

PAIRING: SCOTCH AND SODA

Rarely am I tempted to deliberately recommend a bad pairing for a book, but in this case, that instinct was real. I don't mean bad as in inappropriate or mismatched, but bad as in not pleasing, unsatisfactory, malcontented. This book leaves a burn in your throat, an unpleasant buzz that hits just a little too close to home. Everything is slightly too real, too alive—not a comfortable feeling when reading about a serial killer who leaves glass shards on his victims' eyes. There is no way to talk about this pairing that does not sound gruesome. This is why wine was immediately ruled out as a pairing option. Thank you, but I prefer not to think about the taste of human flesh with fava beans while I'm drinking Chianti. There are many simple, decent options when it comes to self-medicating through this book: a bottle of whiskey, a bottle of gin, a bottle of tequila . . . But if we are not cautious, drinking too much will conjure, rather than banish, these demons, so restraint is preferable. A straightforward scotch and soda is easy to put together, will ease you to sleep after following these nightmarish circumstances, and leaves just enough burn on your tongue to remind you to lock your doors at night.

Along Came a Spider

JAMES PATTERSON

PAIRING: INSIDE JOB

Would it be too much to tell you I was dying to use this drink for a book just like this one? The first crime carried out in this book—the one that sets the stage for all the rest—is an inside job, and the pairing only gets more apt from there. Every character deserves scrutiny in this fast-paced thriller. Alex Cross is one of the best detective protagonists in the history of the genre, and Patterson jumps stylistic tracks at different points in the novel, transitioning fluidly from nauseating serial-killer to the romantic angle to the classic buddy story. This hard-boiled thriller with a softhearted protagonist deserves an equally complex drink, and the Inside Job will do the job in style as well as name.

INGREDIENTS
2 ounces bourbon
½ ounce simple syrup
¼ ounce maraschino liqueur
1 dash absinthe
1 dash Angostura bitters
Maraschino cherry, for garnish
Orange peel, for garnish

INSTRUCTIONS
1. Combine bourbon, simple syrup, maraschino liqueur, absinthe, and Angostura bitters in a cocktail shaker.

2. Top with ice and stir well, 10-15 seconds.

3. Fill an Old Fashioned glass halfway with fresh ice and strain the cocktail into the glass.

4. Garnish with the cherry. Twist the orange peel over the top to release the oil.

Killing Floor
LEE CHILD

Pairing: Whiskey Buck

The antiquated name for a whiskey, ginger, and lime cocktail, a Whiskey Buck is serious enough for Child's bitingly violent story with a touch of sweetness to take the edge off. Child's prose is decisive but engaging, not as blunt as McCarthy nor as descriptive as Follett or Chandler. The cocktail, too, lacks bells and whistles: the quality comes from good ginger ale, good whiskey (not great whiskey—save that for sipping), and a zing of lime. The tale is set in the hot, humid state of Georgia, so the ginger and the lime will revitalize you. But have no fear of nodding off in the afternoon heat. This tale is excellently paced, and your blood pressure will be up by the second chapter. The book—and the drink—will be done before you know it.

INGREDIENTS
2–3 ounces medium quality whiskey (I like Bulleit's bourbon, Johnnie Walker Black, or Knob Creek's entry-level offering)
2–3 ounces ginger ale
Lime wedge, for garnish

INSTRUCTIONS
1. Pour the whiskey into a highball glass filled with ice.

2. Top with ginger ale. Squeeze lime wedge over the top and drop it in.

Note: I am a bit of a ginger ale snob, as the whiskey ginger is one of my favorite cocktails. I don't recommend using ginger beer out of anything plastic unless you're hard up and very thirsty. There are many local companies across America now bottling their own ginger beers; these tend to be much stronger and more flavorful. To do this cocktail the right way, buy a few 12-ounce bottles of a local or smaller producer's ginger beer and use that in your cocktail. When you do it this way, you'll also see why the lime squeeze is essential—it brightens and complements the ginger, two flavors that play together as well in drinks as they do in food.

Tell No One

HARLAN COBEN

PAIRING: ROLLING ROCK

This thriller is not a slow burner. No sir. Within the first two paragraphs you're already wondering who's lying to whom and where their secrets are buried. Set in New York and the surrounding area from New Jersey to Pennsylvania, a new thread of Coben's web is spun outwards on every single page. You'll need to stay sober enough to follow every word Coben drops, every footstep left behind, every clue in every room. A light beer is what we need, something we can nurse as we follow the plot twists. Rolling Rock, the iconic Pennsylvania beer Dr. Beck and his friend Shauna drink to excess one night, touches every social class of the East Coast and is the perfect thing to set the stage from nostalgic summer parties on the shores of Lake Charmaine to Dr. Beck's low-income family practice to the Manhattan offices of the FBI. With two or three bottles of Rolling Rock to lubricate the flow of the pages, you'll be unable to stop yourself from tearing through Beck's furious race to find his Elizabeth—before anyone else finds him first.

The Lovely Bones

ALICE SEBOLD

PAIRING: BLOOD AND SAND

What would a fourteen-year-old girl who has just been raped and murdered by a child molester and a serial killer want to drink in heaven? Probably not a Blood and Sand cocktail, as the name might remind her too starkly of her recent death. But if she did, she might find herself comforted by the sweet blend of scotch, orange juice, and cherry liqueur. This drink's name fits the book, as does the cocktail itself. Susie Salmon's blood is found in soil samples in the field where she was murdered, which is one of the first big clues investigators uncover regarding her disappearance. The Blood and Sand, when done properly, is a heavenly concoction; when improperly made, it's off-balance, sour, and muddy—cocktail hell. To land on the heavenly side, fresh-squeezed orange juice is imperative. (Don't cheat and buy juice. Trust me on this.) Pick a smooth scotch, not a peaty-smoky bottle, and shake the cocktail hard to bring out the froth.

INGREDIENTS

1 ounce scotch
¾ ounce Cherry Heering liqueur
¾ ounce sweet vermouth
¾ ounce fresh-squeezed orange juice
Maraschino cherry, for garnish

INSTRUCTIONS

1. Combine scotch, Cherry Heering, vermouth, and orange juice in a cocktail shaker over ice.

2. Shake very well, 15–20 seconds, and strain into a chilled coupe.

3. Garnish with maraschino cherry.

The Da Vinci Code

DAN BROWN

PAIRING: WHITE ZINFANDEL

This is one of the most popular books in the world, which naturally makes it reviled by literary enthusiasts everywhere. If you've met five people who love *The Da Vinci Code*, you've probably met at least five more who loathe it. But for all its historical inaccuracies and blatant misappropriations of fact, it's a delicious ride. White zinfandel, in many ways an affront to centuries of intentional winemaking tradition, has much in common with Dan Brown's thriller, which is an affront to centuries of historical and religious tradition. Both are frivolous, saccharine, and anti-intellectual. Both leave you with a mild hangover. Both will make you wish you'd made better choices. But if you set aside pretense and enjoy the show, both will delight and entertain. Just don't try to bring a bottle of White zinfandel into the Louvre—the French will have you guillotined for crimes against their culture.

The Girl with the Dragon Tattoo

STIEG LARSSON

PAIRING: AKAVIT

For a book that was titled "Men Who Hate Women" in the native language and features several gruesome murders and a torture chamber worthy of the Inquisition, a drink whose name means "water of life" might sound inappropriate. But the drink works. A Scandinavian spirit similar to vodka but flavored with herbs and spices, *akavit* is known in other countries as *aquavit* or *eaux de vie*. This spirit is to Scandinavians what vodka is to Russians: drunk frequently at meals and almost always at celebrations, usually with an accompanying toast that is both a wish for good health and an expression of trust in your company. Indeed, the tradition of looking your drinking partners in the eye while toasting is said to have descended from the Viking culture of keeping a watchful eye not only on your enemies but your friends as well. This tradition will serve you well as you work through Larsson's frigid thriller. Served cold as a *snaps* (shot) or sipped from a snifter, *akavit* is known to make a heavy meal go down more smoothly. I've discovered it works the same magic for weighty books as it does for large meals. Ask your local liquor store if they stock any Swedish akavit (look for the Skane or Brannvin Special brands) and toss back a *snaps* after this book's haunting prologue—and keep your eye on the Vanger family as you do. *Skal!*

Gone Girl

GILLIAN FLYNN

PAIRING: LAST WORD

With its ominous name and delicate reminder that "the pen is mightier than the sword," the Last Word cocktail fits snugly at the side of this thrilling page-turner, wherein both "victim" and "suspect" are writers and dishonest narrators. The story is told alternately from husband Nick Dunne's perspective, starting the day his wife Amy goes missing, and then from Amy's perspective, through diary entries that explain the history of their relationship. Nick drops little hints along the way that he's leaving out details—he begins to count the number of lies he's told: to the police, to Amy's parents, to his sister. Meanwhile, Amy's diary entries lead us to an illusory understanding of her marriage to Nick. While husband and wife use their words to duel for the reader's trust, make yourself a Last Word before you find out who gets it.

INGREDIENTS

¾ ounce gin
¾ ounce green Chartreuse
¾ ounce lime juice
¾ ounce maraschino liqueur

INSTRUCTIONS

1. Combine all ingredients in a cocktail shaker over ice. Shake well, 10–15 seconds, and strain into a chilled cocktail glass.

DO ANDROIDS DREAM OF ELECTRIC COCKTAILS?
SPECULATIVE AND SCIENCE FICTION

Robots, computers, and spaceships, oh my! Science fiction has been one of the most enduring genres of the last two centuries, beginning when Mary Shelley published her riveting tale of one scientist's arrogance and the lives wrecked as a result. These books do more to reveal our views about our present circumstances than they do to predict the future, but whether as cautionary tale or as crystal ball, science fiction gives us insight into ourselves. Read on to discover the electrifying drinks to enjoy alongside some of our most famous science and speculative fiction novels.

Frankenstein

MARY SHELLEY

PAIRING: CORPSE REVIVER

Cheeky? Maybe. But not only is a Corpse Reviver appropriate for the name alone, it also works historically. The Corpse Revivers #1 and #2 were made famous by Harry Craddock, author of *The Savoy Cocktail Book*, which defined a generation of cocktails for bartenders and drinkers alike. But Craddock's momentous book wasn't published until 1930, and by then Corpse Revivers had been around for decades. In print as early as 1861 in London's *Punch* magazine and probably being consumed many years prior, "Corpse Reviver" is the name given to a family of cocktails originally intended as hangover cures. They were most frequently served to those guilty of the sin of drunkenness—a sin we could accuse Victor Frankenstein of possessing in excess, at least metaphorically. Drunk on power and blinded by revulsion, Victor dooms himself, his hapless creation, and those around him to tragic, grisly deaths. While recovering from the emotional hangover of this mad scientist's delusions, I recommend a Corpse Reviver to summon you—and his creation—back to life.

INGREDIENTS

1 ounce applejack
1 ounce brandy
1 ounce sweet vermouth

INSTRUCTIONS

1. Combine all three ingredients in a cocktail shaker and top the glass with ice.

2. Stir for 10–15 seconds and strain into a chilled cocktail glass.

The Strange Case of Dr. Jekyll and Mr. Hyde

ROBERT LOUIS STEVENSON

PAIRING: IRISH CAR BOMB

Yes, our story takes place in London, not Dublin. No, neither the Irish nor car bombs have anything to do with Stevenson's disturbing Gothic horror. But the drink—name aside—is perfect. As any frat boy can tell you, let an Irish Car Bomb sit for too long after dropping in the shot and the cream will literally curdle. No other cocktail transforms so dramatically, so quickly, from delicious to disgusting. (Well, I may have made some shockingly bad drinks in my early days, but this book is about laboratory successes, not accidents.) This is exactly what happens to the respectable Dr. Jekyll after he takes his transformative potion. Start with a perfectly good character (or beer), add a shot of mysterious potion, and end with a disreputable mess. Our cocktail has one advantage, though—so long as we go bottoms up in time, our concoction will result in a creamy, chocolatey treat, rather than a murderous monster. I'd say we get the better end of the deal.

INGREDIENTS
8 ounces (½ pint) Guinness
¾ ounce Bailey's Irish cream
¾ ounce Irish whiskey

INSTRUCTIONS
1. Fill a cold pint glass half-full with Guinness.

2. Build your depth charge by pouring the Irish cream into a shot glass and topping it with the whiskey.

3. Drop the shot glass into the beer and drink as fast as you can.

The Time Machine

H. G. WELLS

PAIRING: LILLET BLANC

A French liqueur from Bordeaux, Lillet Blanc is an ingredient in a wide variety of cocktails and can also be enjoyed as an aperitif. Apertifs and digestifs were popular during Wells's era, particularly in Europe where the cocktail craze had not yet caught on so ferociously, something similar to Lillet would doubtless have graced his gentleman inventor's dinner parties as he told about his visit to the future. Lillet Blanc is an especially floral drink, evoking lilac, jasmine, and peach blossom, not unlike the flowers poor Weena gives the Time Traveller before he returns to his own time. With a succulent, fruity sweetness balanced by bright acid and heady floral aromas, Lillet Blanc is reminiscent of the Eden-like paradise where our brave adventurer finds himself after traveling more than eight hundred thousand years into the future. Fortunately for us, Lillet has no Morlocks hidden inside the bottle.

Brave New World

ALDOUS HUXLEY

PAIRING: TRIPPY GIN JULEP

Like Neil Gaiman's *American Gods* (page 100), the ideal pairing for this book would be a hit of soma, the stress-relieving, psychedelic pill offered as both tonic and palliative in Aldous Huxley's classic English dystopia. But soma, as Huxley envisions it, is fictional—and the nearest parallels in the real world are highly controlled substances. We can approximte. Spritzy, innocent, and placating, what better to render us slavishly mute in the face of our own pleasure than a fresh and heady Julep with a dash of absinthe to induce a touch of psychosis? With charming flavors like mint and ginger to lift your spirits, plus lime and seltzer to keep you in good health, you, too, will be sedated by Huxley's too-relevant classic.

INGREDIENTS

1 ounce gin
1 ounce absinthe
½ ounce ginger liqueur
½ ounce lime juice
A dozen or so mint leaves, lightly bruised between your palms
3–4 ounces soda water
Lime wedge, for garnish

INSTRUCTIONS

1. Fill a julep cup (or a Collins glass) with fresh crushed ice or whole cubes. Add all ingredients but the soda water. Stir well to mix.

2. Top with the soda water and garnish with the lime wedge.

1984

GEORGE ORWELL

Pairing: The Obituary

This book was particularly difficult to choose a pairing for. Whatever one drinks with this novel must be bleak enough to convey the depths of totalitarianism, cloudy enough to represent the obfuscatory nature of doublethink, boozy enough to carry you into a memory hole of your own, with not a hint of sugary reprieve to be found. The Obituary, a New Orleans cocktail that adds absinthe to a dry martini, will suit our purposes nicely. Although absinthe is traditionally green, I recommend a white absinthe served in a frosted cocktail glass, which will give the drink a milky appearance, as opaque as Big Brother himself. Use a London gin in Orwell's honor, and drink down this cocktail as you read with the uneasy feeling that life really does imitate art.

INGREDIENTS
2 ounces gin
¼ ounce dry vermouth
¼ ounce absinthe

INSTRUCTIONS
1. Combine gin, vermouth, and absinthe in a mixing glass filled with ice.

2. Stir vigorously for 10–15 seconds and strain into a chilled martini glass.

I, Robot

ISAAC ASIMOV

PAIRING: INDIA PALE ALE

It's hard to pinpoint exactly why science fiction makes me think of India pale ales. Possibly it's the freshness and vivacity of the ideas. Possibly it's because IPAs were once a little science fiction themselves. When the British began colonizing India and shipping beer to their dutiful but thirsty expats, they had a devil of a time with spoilage bacteria, which destroyed the beers during the long, hot voyage to India. When George Hodgson's Bow Brewery became the first London brewery to ship barrels of beer without spoilage, using serious quantities of hops as an antimicrobial agent, their sales and exports increased exponentially. Hops, as a preservative, created a beer for the future. Isaac Asimov's collection of interwoven short stories is also a tale of deliberate invention crossbred with unintended consequences. A crisp, light India Pale Ale will keep you buzzing with curiosity as you turn the pages of Asimov's still-relevant reflections on robotics, intelligence, and psychology.

Childhood's End

ARTHUR C. CLARKE

PAIRING: SAISON BEER

A few word changes, a few updates to the technology, and this book could have been written yesterday. In some ways, our fears are very different than they were seventy years ago. In some ways, they are identical. This insightful novel anticipates and discusses many of the same challenges society is facing today—automation, mechanization, universal basic income, socialized support structures, generational divides—but at the same time, those issues are in the background. The central questions are about man's relationship to the alien Overlords, the nature of freedom on a social level, and human evolution. It's a lot of deep thinking, and you'll need something light and refreshing to balance out all the science and philosophy. Something lighthearted and unserious to complement the existential questions and eschatology. Me? I'd crack a *saison*. Lightly hopped for a touch of bitterness, these beers are juicy, crisp, and sometimes just a little funky. The perfect antidote—or complement—to the seriousness of Clarke's tale.

Stranger in a Strange Land

ROBERT HEINLEIN

PAIRING: RED SANGRIA

This sci-fi twist on Christian theology practically begs for a wine pairing. The parallels between the rite of communion and the Martian custom of eating the remains of their "water brothers" who have "discorporated," as well as between the "miracles" Michael performs and the miracles of the Catholic saints, are too striking to avoid. But Heinlein's classic goes well beyond prudish Christian culture. Instead he gives us a lively tale of an alien religious cult based around the ideology of sexuality, polyamory, and universality. We need something lighthearted and fun with a serious backbone. Fruity and charismatic but backed by the intensity of red wine and brandy, sangria fits the bill. Red like the body and blood of our Christ-figure, Mike the Man from Mars, and as seductive as his lifestyle of openness and sexual communion, a lush glass (or pitcher) of sangria is the perfect accompaniment to this neo-spiritual novel of love and awakening.

(*continued on page 74*)

INGREDIENTS

1 pear, cored and sliced

1 apple, cored and sliced

1 orange, sliced into rounds and quartered

4 tablespoons brown sugar

½ cup Spanish brandy

Juice of 2 oranges

Juice of 1 lemon

Juice of 1 lime

1 bottle Spanish red wine (Garnacha preferred)

1 cinnamon stick

1½ cups Spanish *cava*

To garnish, reserve a little of the pear, apple, and orange, and slice into small pieces.

INSTRUCTIONS

1. Combine the pear, apple, and half the orange slices with the brown sugar in a large pitcher and muddle with a muddler or a wooden spoon until the sugar begins to dissolve in the juice.

2. Add the brandy and the lemon, lime, and orange juice and muddle for another 20–30 seconds.

3. Add the red wine and stir to incorporate. Add the cinnamon stick.

4. Cover and refrigerate for a minimum of 2 hours. (Overnight is best.)

5. To serve, fill individual cups with ice and reserved fruit to garnish. Pour sangria into the glasses and top with just enough *cava* to add a little spritz.

A Clockwork Orange

ANTHONY BURGESS

PAIRING: KNIFEY MOLOKO (MILK PUNCH)

This gory exploration of good versus evil and the nature of choice will probably wreak havoc on your digestive system, and you'll be exhausted by the linguistic gymnastics you'll need to perform just to read the thing. Approximate Alex and his droogs' drink of choice with a real-world interpretation of the Knifey Moloko, though our version leaves out the amphetamines and barbiturates. (Add at your own risk.) Does the milk in Alex's favorite drink represent his childish innocence, lost or found? Does the high-octane alcohol percentage get you wondering if there's a seed of evil present in all children that, left to take root, will sprout into a demonic malchickiwick? Does it get you thinking about the fundamental nature of morality as a choice rather than an identity? If you answered *yes* to any of these questions, the drink has done its job. Milk Punch, a sweet and creamy cocktail of repute from days past, is making a resurgence, so we'll feature it here in the hopes it will gently imitate the droogs' Knifey Moloko and revive our spirits after a hard night of reading this book.

INGREDIENTS

1¼ ounces bourbon
½ ounce dark rum
2 ounces whole milk (or cream or half-and-half)
⅛ ounce vanilla extract
½ ounce simple syrup (for a distinct flavor, swap maple syrup)
Fresh-grated nutmeg, for garnish

INSTRUCTIONS

1. Combine all liquid ingredients in a cocktail shaker over ice. Shake vigorously to mix, 10–15 seconds.

2. Strain into a chilled Old Fashioned glass and dust the surface with fresh-ground nutmeg.

Dune

FRANK HERBERT

PAIRING: ARAK

In my humble opinion you'd be hard-pressed to find a more perfect book-and-drink pairing than this. Arak, distilled from grape wine and flavored with the warm spice aniseed, is a traditional Middle Eastern spirit whose name means perspiration or sweat—fitting for a desert planet where sweat is recycled into drinking water and every drop of water must be preserved. It's hard to imagine Herbert didn't think of Arak when brainstorming names for the desert planet Arrakis, where the spice originates and the majority of the action in *Dune* takes place. Rich with spice flavor and traditionally served by diluting with water, Arak may be the closest representation of life on the fictional planet Arrakis we can achieve on planet Earth (without breaking national laws regulating the use of psychoactive substances, that is).

The Left Hand of Darkness

URSULA K. LE GUIN

PAIRING: EISWEIN

Le Guin's revolutionary, decisive act of creativity was *The Left Hand of Darkness*, wherein she deconstructed traditional understandings of gender and paved the path to a different kind of feminism. This novel is set on the frigid and sometimes incomprehensible world of Gethen, where all individuals are ambisexual but for one or two days per month when their sexualities divide into fluid binaries for the purpose of reproduction. Hierarchies of leadership and class exist, but discrimination on the basis of gender is nonexistent. Eiswein, or ice wine, is an ephemeral dessert wine made in the northern winemaking regions of the world at great risk and pain to the winemaker. It, too, is unique in the world. Harvested in early winter, long after the rest of the grapes have been picked, when the berries have frozen on the vine. The sugars, acids, and flavors concentrate as the water freezes out. The setting and writing of *Left Hand* demands something as edifying and complex as eiswein; both tell stories that differ dramatically from the narratives with which we are familiar.

A Scanner Darkly

PHILIP K. DICK

PAIRING: OLIVE OIL MARTINI

Many readers will be disappointed I have not chosen the book of Philip K. Dick's which inspired both this chapter's title and the iconic film "Blade Runner." Sorry, folks, but stay with me. I chose this book for two reasons. First, it's so good, it deserves a little time in the limelight. Second, I want to introduce you to the olive oil cocktail. In *A Scanner Darkly*, PKD introduces us to Bob Arctor and his alter-ego Fred, who reside in the same body. As Fred the law enforcement agent attempts to take down the Substance D drug user Bob Arctor, the two begin swirling around each other and dissociating into disparate personalities, each descending separately into insanity. How are we to replicate this in a drink? Why, with two ingredients that naturally separate and repel: oil and water. Make a dirty martini and scatter a dropper of olive oil over the surface for a pretty and aromatic addition. You might be surprised how much the olive oil changes the drink—and you'll definitely be surprised how much Substance D changes Bob Arctor and Fred over the course of PKD's savage, devastating story.

INGREDIENTS
2½ ounces gin
½ ounce dry vermouth
¼–½ ounce olive brine
1 dropper olive oil
Olive, for garnish

INSTRUCTIONS
1. Combine the first three ingredients in a cocktail shaker and top up with ice.

2. Stir well and strain into a chilled martini glass.

3. Scatter droplets of olive oil across the surface of the cocktail. Garnish with a single olive on a spear or dropped into the drink.

A Hitchhiker's Guide to the Galaxy

DOUGLAS ADAMS

PAIRING: PAN-GALACTIC GARGLE BLASTER

Ever wanted to feel like your brains are being smashed in by a lemon wrapped around a gold brick? No? What's wrong with you? Aren't you an intrepid adventurer, towel at hand, ready to charge through the universe to find the meaning of life, the universe, and everything? No matter—the Pan-Galactic Gargle Blaster, a cocktail introduced in the second book in the series, *The Restaurant at the End of the Universe*, will give you the liquid courage you need to follow Arthur Dent, Ford Prefect, Trillian, and Zaphod Beeblebrox on a never-ending series of hitchhikes around the galaxy. Follow these simple instructions to make the cocktail that is truly out of this world.

INSTRUCTIONS

1. In a Tom Collins glass, combine 1 bottle Ol' Janx Spirit with 1 measure water from the seas of Santraginus V.

2. Drop three properly iced 3 cubes Arcturan Mega-gin into the mixture and allow to melt.

3. Use a Soda Stream to bubble 4 liters of compressed Fallian marsh gas through the mixture.

4. Float a measure of Qualactin Hypermint Extract over the top using the back of a silver spoon.

5. Drop in the tooth of an Algolian Suntiger and wait patiently for it to dissolve.

6. Garnish with a sprinkle of Zamphuor and an olive.

Author's note: Can't seem to find these ingredients at your local liquor store? Maybe you should check the planetary system of Magrathea next time.

Neuromancer

WILLIAM GIBSON

PAIRING: VODKA MARTINI

This sci-fi classic is as sharp as a knife and as cold as ice. There's nothing warm or welcoming about this book. Case, the protagonist and "cyber-cowboy" computer hacker, is a drug addict and a thief; his girlfriend can shoot razors out of her fingers; the bulk of the action centers around cybercrime, the *Neuromancer* equivalent of drug running. The setting shifts from the dirty underbelly of futuristic Japan to dystopian Istanbul to the gleaming metallic space station of Freeside. Whenever I think of hard books with cold edges, I turn to gin or vodka; when I think of slick, smooth storytelling, I want something to suck you down before you can blink. A vodka martini, shaken (or stirred—your preference) over ice and served with a lemon twist, is just the thing to set the stage for Gibson's steely, dynamic writing. Before long, you'll be an accomplice to their crimes.

INGREDIENTS
2 ounces top-shelf vodka such as Grey Goose, Effen, or Pravada
½ ounce dry vermouth
Lemon peel

INSTRUCTIONS
1. Combine vodka and vermouth in a cocktail shaker and top with ice.

2. Shake vigorously (or stir) for 10–15 seconds or until the glass is frosty.

3. Strain into a chilled cocktail glass. Run the lemon peel around the edge of the glass and twist it over the top. Set gently on the side and serve.

Ender's Game

ORSON SCOTT CARD

PAIRING: CLASSIC MARTINI

Though ostensibly about children, there's nothing childish about *Ender's Game*. Ender, the protagonist and the book's namesake, might as well have been born without innocence—and if not, his brother Peter would have immediately stamped it out anyway. Guilty of murder at age six and sent to an elite military school in space a day later as a reward, Ender and his fellow officers-in-training are as cunning, deadly, and vicious as any adults in history. A sci-fi novel set primarily on a space station with very little reference to food or drink, this book was hard to pair. There were no easy answers. Ultimately, I had to return to the pages for inspiration. There, I found the stark excellence of Card's writing, his empathetic but deeply broken characters, and an epic tale taking place on minute scale in the mind of one young boy. Gin called to me (though it should be American, since our protagonists are). I wanted something clean and smooth but cold and cutting. Something with enough alcohol to warm you from the inside, like Valentine, Ender, and his friends. Ultimately, the only choice that fit all my criteria was a classic martini—emblematic, to me, of privileged men in dark places making impossible choices that will ruin many lives. Perhaps we should rename this one the Colonel Graff.

INGREDIENTS

2 ounces gin
½ ounce dry vermouth
Lemon peel, for garnish

INSTRUCTIONS

1. Combine gin and vermouth in a cocktail shaker. Stir until the mixing glass is frosted.

2. Strain into a chilled coupe. Twist the lemon peel over the cocktail and place it on the edge of the glass.

Children of Men

P. D. JAMES

PAIRING: WINE, DEALER'S CHOICE

Less science fiction and more speculative fiction—there's no scientific explanation given for the sudden fertility crisis, nor for why one woman out of so many manages to get pregnant. Some might think the best pairing for this book would be a drink that promises fertility, but all the characters in this novel would laugh. All those remedies have been tried. All scientific advances have been put to the test and failed. No, the drink for this book must be more than an herbal remedy, more than a doctor's promises. It must be literal magic, luck so good it comes from a leprechaun—a miracle so obvious it makes the coldest atheist stir with belief, as surely as Mohammad's ascension to heaven or Jesus's walk on water. Unfortunately for you, I am neither wizard nor saint, so I can deliver neither miracle nor magic. But we can come close. The story of Jesus turning water into wine is as miraculous (to a wine-lover) as they come, and, in this case, goes hand-in-hand with the very British tradition of celebrating a new birth by "wetting the baby's head"—downing any number of drinks at a local pub. Celebrate the miracle of birth with a drink that is downright miraculous: a bottle of your favorite fermented grape juice.

Snow Crash

NEAL STEPHENSON

PAIRING: RAMOS GIN FIZZ

Does science fiction imagine the future? Or does it create the future? The classic sci-fi writers of the '40s and '50s, so concerned with alien first contact and terraforming Mars, never bothered to predict the massively interconnected computing power of the iPhone or Android. But then how did Stephenson anticipate the assembly-line production of code for corporate software? Or the untraceable digital currency which vaguely resembles Bitcoin? We'll leave those questions for the philosophers. Made properly, a Ramos Gin Fizz creates a delicate, snow-like foam on the top and takes almost as long to make as it will take you to read the book. Drink a few of these while pondering the questions about language, human nature, and the future of society posed in this book, and before long, you'll have the all the answers.

INGREDIENTS

2 ounces gin
1 dash orange blossom water
1 egg white
½ ounce half-and-half
½ ounce lemon juice
½ ounce lime juice
½ ounce simple syrup
1 ounce soda water

INSTRUCTIONS

1. Combine all but the last ingredient in a cocktail shaker and shake vigorously, without ice, for 20–30 seconds.

2. Top up your shaker with ice and shake for another 30 seconds.

3. Gently strain into a chilled Collins glass. Slowly, so as not to lose too much carbonation, pour soda water into the shaker to rinse. Slowly pour the soda water and foam into the cocktail. Serve.

Ready Player One
ERNEST CLINE

PAIRING: CORPSE REVIVER NO. BLUE

Sifting through all the eighties references and nerd factoids to find the right drink for *Ready Player One* was so exhausting that it took me forever to realize I had missed the point. *Ready Player One* might *seem* like it's a book about the eighties, so thick is the pop culture, but in reality, this is a near-future dystopia about corporate monopolies, government corruption, and skyrocketing economic inequality. When you strip away the gleeful references to Pac-Man and Star Trek, what remains has more in common with *Blade Runner* than *Back to the Future*. What we're after, then, is a gritty drink with a thin veneer of optimism. A Corpse Reviver No. Blue, created as a twist on the traditional Corpse Reviver cocktails by a Bacardi brand ambassador named Jacob Briars, goes heavy on the alcohol and light on the blue, and will therefore suit our purposes nicely.

INGREDIENTS
1 ounce gin
1 ounce blue curaçao
1 ounce Lillet Blanc
1 ounce lemon juice
1 dash absinthe
Lemon twist

INSTRUCTIONS
1.   Combine all ingredients in a shaker, top with ice, and shake well.

2.   Strain into a chilled glass and garnish with a lemon twist to serve.

Author's note: If you're wondering why this book is in the Sci-Fi section instead of the Young Adult section, name me a kid under twenty-five who would understand all the references to '80s culture in Ready Player One.

LIZARD'S LEG AND OWLET'S WING
MAGIC POTIONS FOR SWORDS AND SPELLS

Fantasy does the same thing as science fiction, but in the opposite direction. Hearkening to the days of yore, when the world was less known and magic seemed to lurk around every corner, these books tell us about ourselves by revealing our deepest wishes and our darkest fears. For these books we'll be looking for the drinks of yore, too—stout beers for stout hearts, wines as clear as a clarion call. Here you'll find the ancient magic of potion-making made modern by clever use of herbs, chemistry, and biology, used to bring dragons and demons to life.

Dracula,

BRAM STOKER

PAIRING: BLOODY MARY

Would it have been possible to pair any other drink with this classic Gothic horror? Not to mention what happens to the poor girl named Mary halfway through the book. . . . Let's just say you'll want a stiff pour of vodka, topped up with loads of Worcestershire and plenty of garlic. Just because we're reading about vampires doesn't mean we want to invite them in for tea.

Note: This particular incarnation emphasizes the tomato-pepper-Worcestershire flavors without much heat, because no one has seen any evidence that vampires enjoy hot sauce. If you'd like to add a dose of spice, I recommend the Secret Aardvark Habanero Hot Sauce—in my mind, the best Bloody Mary hot sauce on the market.

INGREDIENTS

2 ounces vodka
4 ounces tomato juice
½ ounce fresh lemon juice
¼ teaspoon horseradish (freshly grated, if possible)
¼ teaspoon freshly minced garlic
3–4 dashes Worcestershire sauce
Lemon wedge, for garnish
Celery stick, for garnish
Fresh cracked pepper, for garnish

INSTRUCTIONS

1. Combine all ingredients in a cocktail shaker and shake vigorously for 10–15 seconds to mix.

2. Strain over ice in a highball glass. Squeeze a lemon wedge over the top, and drop it in.

3. Crack fresh pepper over the top, to taste, and garnish with a celery stick.

Another Note: My favorite way to enjoy a Bloody Mary is with plenty of other odds and ends—including, but not limited to: pickled peppers, cornichons, onions, garlic, green beans, olives, and more. If you're serving to a book club or large group, feel free to include several options so that guests may garnish as they like.

The Fellowship of the Ring

J. R. R. TOLKIEN

Pairing: English Ale

If this book were not explicitly about drinks, I would not hesitate to recommend a good selection of "pipe-weed" or tobacco leaf as the perfect pairing for Tolkien's seminal fantasy series starring halflings as the unlikely heroes. We may not be lucky enough to find an untapped keg from the Green Dragon in Hobbiton or a mug of Barliman Butterbur's most excellent ale, but we can do our best. A sturdy English ale like a Newcastle or a Sam Smith will carry you from the sign of the Prancing Pony to the welcoming halls of Rivendell and through the dark chasms of Moria. To really get into the spirit, find a local English pub and bring your copy to the bar. After a pint (or four), stand up on the bartop and start singing one of Bilbo's songs. The guests are sure to be impressed, so long as you avoid disappearing mid-song.

The Once and Future King

T. H. WHITE

PAIRING: CÔTES DU RHÔNE

Despite Disney's best efforts to convince us otherwise, this is not a children's book. The beginning is impish and innocently comedic, but later sections take on a darker aspect. But the pairing for this book is simple enough. White ostensibly set the book in the fourteenth century in England, a time when drinking water was spurned as unhealthy, beer was for the common peasants, and wine was for the kings and nobles. There, we've narrowed it down—we must have some kind of wine for our *Once and Future King*. But what kind of wine? Well, the English at the time were mostly drinking wines from the Côtes du Rhône, and red wine is kingly enough for Arthur. Wines from the northern region of the Rhone valley, where they specialize in meaty, austere Syrahs, would make the perfect accompaniment. But in the fourteenth century, even kings had to take what they could get. Don't be too picky about this one—find a producer you like and call it good. After all, even King Arthur was probably drinking little more than alcoholic vinegar.

Dragonflight

ANNE MCCAFFREY

PAIRING: KLAHKTAIL

Klah, a restorative and invigorating drink made from tree bark and consumed warm, often with sweetener or cream, is the primary drink mentioned in *The Dragonriders of Pern* series. And although the tree whose bark is used to make klah is native to Pern (therefore not available on good ol' Earth), Anne McCaffrey has offered us some helpful clues as to how it tastes so we can invent our own: "The flavor is something like cinnamony chocolate, with a touch of hazelnut and coffee." In McCaffrey's honor, I've concocted a warm hazelnut-and-coffee cocktail with Irish whiskey, after McCaffrey's place of origin, that will serve as our Earthly klah imitation I call the Klahktail.

INGREDIENTS
2 ounces milk
Cinnamon stick
2 ounces Jameson's Irish whiskey
2 ounces Kahlúa
1 ounce Frangelico
Whipped cream, for topping

INSTRUCTIONS:
1. Bring several cups of water to a boil. Then pour it into your serving glasses or mugs to warm them.

2. Over low heat, in a thick-bottomed pan, warm the milk and cinnamon stick to a simmer. Stir constantly to avoid burning the milk.

3. Empty hot water from your serving glass. Remove the milk from heat and pour into the warmed glass.

4. Add whiskey, Kahlúa, and Frangelico and stir well to mix.

5. Top with whipped cream and sprinkle with cinnamon. Serve hot.

Interview with the Vampire
ANNE RICE

PAIRING: SIDECAR

Hailing from the city of New Orleans and with a name to emphasize
Louis's role as "sidecar" to Lestat, this cocktail will bring Anne Rice's
unforgettable vampire novel to life in a whole new way. Incorporating
French cognac in honor of Lestat's heritage and a sporting a long history
dating back to the 1860s, this cocktail will help you power through a long
night of recording (or reading) the vampire Louis's story.

INGREDIENTS
2 ounces cognac
1 ounce lemon juice
1 ounce Cointreau
Lemon slice, for the sugar rim
Sugar, for garnish

INSTRUCTIONS
1. Run a slice of lemon around the rim of a
   chilled cocktail shaker. (Discard the lemon
   slice.) Turn the glass upside down in a small
   plate or bowl dusted with sugar to rim the
   glass with sugar.

2. Combine all ingredients in a separate cocktail
   glass. Shake over ice until glass frosts over,
   10–15 seconds.

3. Strain into the sugar-rimmed glass.

The Sword of Shannara

TERRY BROOKS

Pairing: Sour beer

Fantastic act of plagiarism or genius work of fantasy? Why not both? Terry Brooks's epic fantasy series borrows at least as much from J. R. R. Tolkien's *Lord of the Rings* as it invents on its own, but that doesn't make the experience less immersive or inspiring. Still, if you're a little sour on ideological theft, this beer's the one for you; by contrast, if you revere Brooks's work, this is still the beer for you, as sour beers are delicious, thirst-quenching, and rapidly growing in popularity. Many beers served and drunk in the fantasy worlds of this section would undoubtedly have been a little sour, though not intentionally: the tart, acidic character of these brews comes from a combination of acetic and lactic acid–producing bacteria. These beers were the "original" beers, as all beers were once fermented "wild," before isolated, cultivated yeasts were available to brewers. As to whether modern brewers are plagiarizing or reinventing the genre—who's to judge, so long as the beer is good? Same for the book, I say.

The Mists of Avalon

MARION ZIMMER BRADLEY

PAIRING: MEAD

For this feminist retelling of the legends of King Arthur, we need a drink that reminds us of a time when goddess worship was still prevalent, when women and men sat equally at the thrones of the gods, before the corrupting notion of original sin tainted our perception of the feminine. Mead is that drink. Mead, or honey-wine, is honey that has been fermented into an alcoholic beverage in a process nearly identical to winemaking, and is one of the oldest alcoholic beverages in existence. It has a long history throughout Europe, Africa, and Eurasia, and features prominently in Norse and Germanic mythology, as well as in the Vedic and Hindu religions of the Indian subcontinent. Indeed, the legendary poet-bard Taliesin, who appears in *The Mists of Avalon* as a Merlin, wrote a poem about mead: the *Kanu y Med*, or "Song of Mead." When you drink mead, you're drinking mythology. You're drinking ancient history. Drink sweet honey-wine from the sacred chalice, and let the Huntress, the Goddess, the Priestess tell you her story.

Mort

TERRY PRATCHETT

PAIRING: PORTER BEER

Picking one of Terry Pratchett's books to feature was an enormous challenge. After all, there are forty-one books in the Discworld series alone. The only reason I picked *Mort* was because it was the only one I had a copy of at home. Luckily, *Mort* is one of his most popular works, and despite not having read any Terry Pratchett before this book, I was instantly entranced. It only took a few pages before I grew thirsty, and I knew immediately what I wanted: Porter beer. Porter is the perfect accompaniment to *Mort*. These beers are dark in flavor but lighthearted in texture, as stolid as the namesake character, and dense enough to get you through an apprenticeship with Death. The book is short—a quick reader might finish it in just over two pints. (Yes, a pint of beer is a unit of measurement now.)

The Eye of the World,

ROBERT JORDAN

Pairing: Loire Valley Chenin Blanc

A massive epic that crosses generations and renders magic and mythology equally tactile, Robert Jordan's *Wheel of Time* series has been hailed as the greatest fantasy series since *The Lord of the Rings* and probably has only been matched to date by *A Game of Thrones*. It's a story that requires you to be committed for the long haul—indeed, if you started when the first book was published, you had to wait twenty-two years to discover the ending. There's such a sparkle in this book, the sheen of groomed horses, red pennants, and silvery armor, that I quickly realized we need something uplifting, glittering. Wines made from the Chenin Blanc variety hailing from France's Loire Valley are just what we need. With powerful acidity and delicate fruit and white flower aromas, these wines have a charisma and sparkle befitting Jordan's invented world. It helps that the Loire *feels* like the Westlands. The Loire Valley wine country is dotted with magnificent castles, glittering spires, and elegant bridges, nestled in a long, wide berth as the river runs to the ocean. It's a paradise that makes you feel like you've stepped into a fantasy novel. What more could you want?

Assassin's Apprentice

ROBIN HOBB

PAIRING: CHOCOLATE STOUT

There's such a brooding sense of reality in this fantasy world, the introductory chapter of Robin Hobb's *Farseer* trilogy and her larger *Realm of the Elderlings*, and it seems to call for a dark and serious drink. FitzChivalry has a rough time of it growing up, between loneliness, social isolation, and the complex politics of palace drama. Fitz's solace is often in the Wit, a type of magic that allows him to bond deeply and emotionally with animals—but this type of magic is reviled and mistrusted by his human companions. His relationship with the royal hunting dogs, in particular the puppy Nosy, become a source of joy and delight throughout the book. That's why the pairing is a chocolate stout—not for the dogs, we don't want them eating chocolate—but to give our dark brew a sweet, succulent aspect, just like Fitz's relationship with the animals around him brings a joyful vivacity to this brooding fantasy in a way that only animals can.

A Game of Thrones

GEORGE R. R. MARTIN

PAIRING: BAROLO OR BARBARESCO

Short of distilled spirits or liqueurs, it's difficult to imagine an alcoholic beverage that wouldn't pair well with George R. R. Martin's bloody tale of clashing clans. Beer, wine, and mead are all mentioned repeatedly and in myriad forms. There are some more unique fermented beverages—at least to the Western palate—fermented mare's milk, for example, the favored intoxicant of the Dothraki. Any of these drinks would serve adequately as a pairing, but the match made in heaven (or in the Godswood) must be Piedmontese Barolo or Barbaresco. Here's why. For this first book in the *Game of Thrones* series—the one for which we seek a perfect pairing—the bulk of the action takes place in King's Landing. If one were to overlay a map of Westeros onto a map of Europe, it follows that Winterfell and the Northern lands are (roughly speaking) the British Isles, Riverrun and the Vale of Arryn are France, and King's Landing, the seat of the Holy Sept and the Iron Throne, is Rome. Although things change dramatically throughout the series, in this inaugural book we find a tale full of lords and ladies, displays of wealth, and courtly intrigue. The wine we drink should be as noble as the characters, complex as their schemes, and red as the blood they spill. Nebbiolo, the grape from which Barolos and Barbarescos are made, results in wines as sultry and rich as Cersei Lannister but as proud and fiery as Ned Stark. They are some of the finest wines produced in Italy, and carry us back before Italian unification, when the principalities warred like wolves for political and economic status—which sounds like *A Game of Thrones*. Enjoy a bottle of this sumptuous wine as you settle in with this epic and bloodthirsty tale, and you'll soon find yourself at a new level of understanding with everyone's favorite dwarf.

Storm Front

JIM BUTCHER

PAIRING: BLUE COSMOPOLITAN

The first in the *Dresden Files* series, *Storm Front* is a delightful, colorful mishmash of just about every fantasy and P.I. noir trope in modern fiction. Although the novel is rife with heavy-handed themes of mob violence, drug trafficking, and cops-versus-robbers, it never manages to feel serious. To the contrary, it's like a superhero movie: pure entertainment from beginning to end. Butcher's mockery of magic and mayhem screams for a vibrant pairing—we want something as rollicking as our story. Get your rocks off during this smashing ride with this delightful, colorful mishmash of a cocktail: a blue Cosmopolitan, with curaçao and enough sweetness for Harry Dresden's old-fashioned chivalry, brings Butcher's delightful nerd-fantasy to life in all its weird and wild glory.

INGREDIENTS
1 ounce vodka
1 ounce white cranberry juice
1 ounce blue curaçao
Squeeze of lime
Lemon peel, for garnish

INSTRUCTIONS
1. Combine all liquid ingredients in a cocktail shaker. Top with ice and shake well, 10–15 seconds.

2. Strain into a chilled martini glass.

3. Twist the lemon peel over the top and drop in for garnish.

American Gods

NEIL GAIMAN

PAIRING: JACK DANIEL'S AND COFFEE

The perfect thing to drink with Neil Gaiman's inventive tale of modern mythology would really be a bottle of soma, the distilled plant essence of some lost ancient herb that was used in Vedic mythology to grant the drinker godlike status, or immortality. The Hindu gods and heroes thrived on this substance, in addition to the offered prayers from their devoted followers. But since no one is able to agree on precisely what the origins of ancient soma are, it's quite unattainable these days. Another option might be ambrosia, the sustaining nectar of the Greek gods, or even the liquified essence of prayers, offerings, and worship sent to you by devoted followers of your own small religion. But seeing as modern alchemists have yet to distill thoughts and prayers into anything tangible, let alone drinkable, we'll have to settle for next best: Jack Daniel's and coffee.

Why, you ask? Both are mentioned frequently in the book, and, according to American mythology, are as quintessentially American as they come. Wednesday, arguably the book's main character, constantly exudes the smell of Jack Daniel's, and there's a Native American character whose name, in fact, is Whiskey Jack. Coffee, too, is mentioned with curious frequency, as the characters skip from diner to diner, from odd road-side attraction to even odder roadside attraction, on sleepless nights and long drives through the mythical locales of deep Americana. The pairing works: both drinks are bitter, dark, and warming—enough to make you scowl, but also to warm you through the cold pages of a Midwestern winter. So pour yourself a cup of coffee—the greasier the mug, the better—with a shot of Jack Daniel's, and prepare yourself for a brutal ride through the seedy underbelly of myth, murder, and madness.

Jonathan Strange and Mr. Norell

SUSANNA CLARKE

PAIRING: MAGICAL MARTINI

Here is a book that calls for a truly magical drink. Between feats of spell-casting not dreamed of in the wizarding world of Harry Potter—raising the dead and summoning familiars—and intense collaboration and competition between two of the greatest magicians in (alternate) history, the Messrs Gilbert Norell and Jonathan Strange do not shy from the dramatic. Although they might object to parlor tricks or sleight-of-hand, this martini is neither. It's honest-to-goodness, real-life magic—in our world, better known as science. The unique ingredient in this cocktail is butterfly pea flower extract, which is native to Thailand and Malaysia and changes color dramatically from blue to pink and violet when in a low-pH environment. It's a striking change, almost as shocking as traveling to the land of Faerie or discovering you've been awoken from the dead.

INGREDIENTS

1½ ounces English gin (Beefeater's or Tanqueray works well here)
¾ ounce ginger liqueur
½ ounce simple syrup
1 dropper b'Lure butterfly pea flower extract (available for order online)
¾ ounce lemon juice
Edible flowers, for garnish
Lemon wheel, for garnish

INSTRUCTIONS

1. Combine all ingredients but the lemon juice, wheel, and flowers in a cocktail shaker.

2. Top with ice and shake well to mix.

3. Add lemon juice slowly and watch the drink change color. Garnish with edible flowers and wedge the lemon wheel on the side of the glass.

The Name of the Wind,

PATRICK ROTHFUSS

PAIRING: BARLEYWINE

The name is deceptive: barleywine is actually beer. Intense, aromatic, brooding beer. Just the sort of thing to get you through the long night you're about to spend at the pub listening to Kvothe the Kingkiller. Like any beer, barleywine is made from a mash of grains. But more grains are packed into the original mash to achieve a higher potential alcohol, and the resulting sweetness from the sugar extraction needs to be balanced with a proportional increase in hops. With a broad palate shape, brooding aromatics, and an extended finish, barleywine is capable of being cellared like good wine and is often bottled by vintage rather than batch. It makes you think of dark pubs, firesides, and men in cloaks. It makes you think of swords and stories. It makes you think of an innkeeper pulling a dusty bottle of his finest when a special guest comes calling. Whether you're a longtime fan of Patrick Rothfuss or taking your first crack at *The Name of the Wind*, you'll be glad to have a nourishing bottle of barleywine near at hand as you follow Kvothe's long and winding path to vengeance.

The Way of Kings

BRANDON SANDERSON

PAIRING: GERMAN RIESLING

A kingly wine for a kingly book—though many of the characters herein are far from nobility. Sanderson's invented world of Cosmere is shockingly creative and comes vibrantly to life. His characters, too, whether heroes by innate ability or stubborn will, are clear and compelling despite their faults. For these feats of fantasy, we need a magical wine. Germany's Mosel and Rhineland regions produce Rieslings of power and finesse; with such austere charisma it's a wonder the farmers who make them aren't kings themselves. But that narrative fits within our pairing, as nobility of character is often incongruous with nobility of birthright in Sanderson's world, and these winemakers and farmers, often the same families for generations on end, are unusually content with their agrarian lifestyle.

A Discovery of Witches

DEBORAH HARKNESS

PAIRING: CHAMPAGNE, BLANC DE NOIRS

The art of crafting cocktails has been referred to as a sort of alchemy, in which disparate ingredients are combined to make something that tastes like liquid gold and gives the drinker health and a long life (according to salesmen, anyway). But true medieval alchemy, the kind that features so prominently in Deborah Harkness's *All Souls* trilogy, involves a different kind of alchemy: a marriage of opposites, the union between light and dark, the sun and the moon, masculine and feminine. Alchemy is the long and tribulating process of distilling base substances such as lead into the spiritually pure element of gold and in the process achieving eternal life. It requires many transmutations, distillations, and fermentations. And although Champagne doesn't involve any distillation, it's about as close to liquid gold as we can get. Sparkling blanc de noirs are made from the dark-skinned pinot noir grapes, as opposed to chardonnay or a blend of the two. To make blanc de noirs, pinot noir is picked early, while it retains its youthful acidity. The grapes are pressed immediately to avoid color extraction from the skins. It's fermented first into a still wine, and is then bottled with an extra bit of sugar and yeast, which creates a secondary fermentation in the bottle. This gives it the creamy bubbles and warm yeasty aromas—not to mention the brilliantly gold color. By choosing French Champagne, we're honoring the de Clermont family and their love of luxurious wine (although Matthew tends to prefer reds, for obvious reasons). If the time-consuming, multistage process of turning pinot noir grapes into golden, life-giving bottles of Champagne doesn't sound like an alchemical marriage to you, I guess eternal life and wealth will be forever beyond your reach.

The Night Circus

ERIN MORGENSTERN

PAIRING: CHAMPAGNE COCKTAIL

For this book we need something that sparkles and glitters at every turn, shining as brilliantly as the Cirque du Rêves. A champagne cocktail, made with brandy, bitters, a sugar cube, and—obviously—champagne, brings its own dazzle to *The Night Circus*. It's a cosmopolitan drink, fitting for the Cirque du Rêves world tour. It's also a romantic drink, just sweet enough to tease, evoking the star-crossed meet-cute between Marco and Celia in Paris. With a single bottle of champagne, you can make between four and six cocktails, and you can even prepare them in advance for ease of serving. A batch of these served at book club to pair with Morgenstern's epic debut will dazzle as surely as the feats of magic Celia and Marco perform through their competitive, glamorous tour of the world.

INGREDIENTS (FOR 1 COCKTAIL)
1 sugar cube
2–3 dashes Angostura bitters
1 ounce brandy
4–6 ounces champagne
Orange slice, for garnish
Maraschino cherry, for garnish

INSTRUCTIONS
1. Drop the sugar cube in the bottom of a chilled champagne flute.

2. Add the bitters on top to saturate, and follow with the brandy.

3. Slowly, so as not to lose too much carbonation, top with champagne.

4. Garnish with orange slice and maraschino cherry.

Note: To prepare in advance, simply omit step 3. Chill the glasses in the refrigerator, and top with the champagne right before serving. A bottle of champagne has approximately twenty-five servings, so you should be able to comfortably make six cocktails with one bottle using a 4-ounce pour.

SWOON-WORTHY
DRINKS FOR LOVERS OF LOVE

Liquors were long used medicinally to treat a variety of illnesses. They were often used to revive women from fainting spells or fits of "nerves." While we now know those diagnoses were almost entirely bogus, that shouldn't stop us from using a brandy or two to revive us from a swoon over the gallant obstinacy of one Mr. Fitzwilliam Darcy. The drinks that dine and dance with these lovely books are intended to play up the romance, bring out the drama, and serve as aphrodisiacs as we fall in love with our favorite characters and stories over and over again.

Romeo and Juliet

WILLIAM SHAKESPEARE

PAIRING: RECIOTO DELLA VALPOLICELLA

"A glooming peace this morning with it brings," which is why we're drinking Recioto, a lovely but serious red wine made from dried grapes, rather than prosecco, a bright sparkling wine also from nearby Verona, as we read Shakespeare's heart-wrenching tale of doomed lovers. In addition to serving as the backdrop for Romeo and Juliet's misadventured affair, Verona is located in the province of Veneto, where the sumptuous, sweet wine Recioto della Valpolicella has been made for centuries just up the river Adige and would have been served to courtiers such as those from the noble houses of Capulet and Montague. The practice of allowing grape clusters to dry before fermentation, thus concentrating the sugar and flavor, is an ancient one, praised by writers and wine lovers from Homer to Pliny the Elder. With sweetness to lift your heart as Romeo woos Juliet but color and maturity to carry you through the bloody, bitter ending, Recioto marries theme and tradition in honor of our star-crossed lovers who never made it to the altar.

Pride and Prejudice

JANE AUSTEN

PAIRING: RUM PUNCH

You're probably frowning right now as you remember the dark days of college drinking, when frat-party punch more closely resembled canned fruit cocktail than it did anything classy enough to match Austen's Regency-era romance. But long before impoverished college students corrupted punch with bottom-shelf plastic-bottle liquor, this fruity, boozy drink was fancy enough to be served at dinner and dance parties, much like the ones Elizabeth and Jane Bennet attend while courting or fending off various suitors. Rum punch celebrates the English imperial triumphs of naval dominance and sugarcane production—a distant backdrop of Austen's novel, which features several chivalrous (or not) military men of the infamous British army. Put on your white satin gloves, pour yourself a glass of punch, and let Messrs Bingley and Darcy carry you around the dance floor. And don't fret if you left your witty repartée at home—Elizabeth has enough to share.

INGREDIENTS [FOR 8–10 SERVINGS]

4 pints water

1 pound raw cane sugar

3 lemons, juiced, with the rinds

1 (750 mL) bottle dark rum

1 (750 mL) bottle ruby port

1 apple, sliced

1 orange, peeled, pieces separated but intact

1 cup sliced fresh pineapple (optional)

INSTRUCTIONS

1. Combine the water, sugar, and lemon juice and rinds in a saucepan. Bring to a boil.

2. After it has boiled, cool the mixture, either in the refrigerator or in an ice bath if you're in a hurry, and strain out the lemon pieces.

3. Combine the rum and port in a punch bowl.

4. Mix in the sugar solution. Top with slices of apples, oranges, and pineapple (if using).

5. To serve, fill punch glasses or tumblers with ice, and ladle punch over the top.

Jane Eyre
CHARLOTTE BRONTË

Pairing: Tawny Port

Swoon-worthy indeed! The reclusive, brooding Rochester has inspired generations of devoted romance fans, but even more so has the fierce, headstrong titular character garnered love and admiration from women the world over. This book is more than a love story, but it is a love story at its core: a woman's quest to love herself, and in the process, to love a mercurial but devoted man. (Never mind the first wife stowed away in the attic.) Tawny port is a swoon-worthy beverage, the mature older sibling of the more juvenile ruby port. Both styles hail from Portugal, from the Douro. The difference lies in the aging process: ruby port is aged in reductive environments of concrete or stainless-steel holding tanks, to preserve the red color and the youthful vivacity, while tawny is allowed to oxidize in wooden barrels, taking on oak and oxidative flavor characters as well as a creamy, voluptuous mouthfeel. These ports are as Byronic as Edward Rochester but as pure and independent as Jane Eyre. Like the book, a good bottle of tawny port will only improve with age.

Anna Karenina

LEO TOLSTOY

PAIRING: SAUTERNES

How do the Russians manage to write such tragic stories in such exuberant prose? Every time I read Tolstoy and Dostoyevsky, this question dominates my thoughts. In this book and in Dostoyevsky's *The Brothers Karamazov*, the buoyancy of the tone defies comprehension in the face of the subject matter. Well, at any rate. By now you're probably wondering why you should be drinking a sweet dessert wine from France with a Russian tragic romance. Why not just throw back a cold glass of vodka? Tempting, surely. But such a straightforward pairing wouldn't have done the tempestuous Princess Anna Karenina justice. Nor does it capture the astonishing breadth of this novel. Sauternes, a world-famous dessert-style wine, is as effusive as Tolstoy's prose but as intoxicating as Anna and Vronsky's affair. Made primarily from the Semillon grape (with a little Sauvignon Blanc and Muscadelle in the mix, depending on the producer) in the Graves district of Bordeaux, this wine is made partly by yeast and partly by fungus: *Botrytis cinerea*, or "noble rot." This fungus helps to dehydrate the grapes, concentrate sugars and flavors, reduce acidity, and add viscosity. The result is transcendent: a supple, luxurious, deeply aromatic wine. We need not abandon hope of connecting the pairing historically as well as thematically to our subject: Sauternes, along with champagne, was extremely popular with the Russian imperial court, and would undoubtedly have found its way into the glasses of our aristocratic young lovers. Last, but not least: can you think of a better way to describe Anna and Vronsky's affair than "noble rot"?

Lady Chatterley's Lover

D. H. LAWRENCE

PAIRING: OREGON CHARDONNAY

Disconnected though they may be in historical time and place, one sip of these creamy, sensual white wines will put you in the mind of Constance Chatterley's sexual adventures with her lover. Oregon chardonnays are bright and full-bodied with a crisp, mouthwatering bite of acid. There's a touch of reservation there, too—a hint of a pause, a breath of anticipation, in the finest Oregon chards. At their best, these white wines can be almost erotic themselves: succulent, juicy, and as generous as a lover. D. H. Lawrence's prose works the same way, reveling in freedom and possibility as he pushes and blurs class boundaries and social structures in prim British society. One taste of these vivacious wines will leave you thirsty for more, so find a bottle and let yourself be seduced by chardonnay and Lady Chatterley at the same time.

Rebecca

DAPHNE DE MAURIER

PAIRING: THE JASMINE

Alcohol is rarely mentioned in this subtle romantic thriller, but that was no obstacle to finding the perfect pairing. It presented itself early on in the novel, when Maxim de Winters explains to the future second Mrs. de Winters that, "the only form of intoxication that appealed to him" was that of the scent of flowers. The pairing was born. Enticingly romantic but layered throughout with unease, suspense, and malcontent, *Rebecca* demands a pairing as charming as the first Mrs. de Winters but as un-settling as Mrs. Danvers. The Jasmine, a modern classic—like the book under consideration—is floral and seductive, beautiful but deadly. Gin is the primary alcohol, balanced by small proportions of Campari and Cointreau. Luscious notes of orange blossom, raspberry, and fragrant rose petal characterize this drink, but the gin pour is not for the faint of heart. Neither is the book.

INGREDIENTS
2 ounces gin
¾ ounce fresh lemon juice
¼ ounce Campari
¼ ounce Cointreau
Thin twist of lemon peel, for garnish
Nasturtium or other edible flower, for garnish

INSTRUCTIONS

1. Combine all ingredients except the flower and lemon peel in a cocktail shaker and top with ice. Shake vigorously.

2. Strain into a chilled coupe and lay the lemon twist along the rim.

3. Set the flower gently in the center of the cocktail, or, if you prefer, prop it against the side of the glass with the lemon twist.

Doctor Zhivago

BORIS PASTERNAK

PAIRING: WHITE RUSSIAN

According to Urban Dictionary, this book's namesake cocktail is a vodka-Dr Pepper concoction, and I hope you won't mix yourself anything of the sort. This artful novel deserves better. While the White Russian cocktail in pop culture might make us think more of the Dude and his missing rug than the October Revolution, this drink has the vodka for our Russian drama, milk to nourish you through the long, dark winters, and the name to evoke the bloody conflict between the Whites and the Reds in the aftermath of the Bolshevik revolution. A little sweet and a little creamy, this drink can be romantic, too—reminiscent of the beautiful Lara, and Yuri's love for her against all odds. Let it warm you through the cold season; let it charm you through war and revolution. Am I talking about the book or the drink? Does it matter?

INGREDIENTS
2 ounces vodka (preferably Russian)
1 ounce Kahlúa
Float of heavy cream (1–2 ounces, to taste)

INSTRUCTIONS
1. Fill an Old Fashioned glass with ice and top with the vodka and Kahlúa.

2. Float the heavy cream on top. Stir well to mix. (Or, if you like how it looks in the glass before mixing, leave the cream for a minute or two to sink, and serve.)

The Princess Bride

WILLIAM GOLDMAN

PAIRING: CHIANTI CLASSICO

After you've defeated the vengeful Spaniard in a fencing match and over-come rhyme master Fezzik in hand-to-hand combat, you can finally sit down and share a glass of wine with your long-lost lover—so long as you've built up a healthy tolerance to iocane powder, of course. Most people know the film version of this story; far fewer know how great the original book truly is. Written like the comedic rebuttal to Romeo and Juliet, Goldman's timeless tale of star-crossed lovers is set in the fictional Renaissance-era province of Florin. For this pairing, we have a Florentine wine for our lovers from Florin: Chianti, made from the Sangiovese vari-ety, is produced in the hills and valleys of the Tuscan countryside. During the Renaissance era, the wine trade was vital to the Florentine market, and wines from the surrounding region of Tuscany, as well as foreign mar-kets such as Crete and Corsica, passed through Florence on their way to wealthy merchants in Northern Europe. By the peak of the Renaissance in the 16th and 17th centuries, Florentine wines were renowned throughout Europe as some of the finest in existence. It's important to note that the wines grown and produced in Italy at the time were very different from the wines grown today—Sangiovese, which is now virtually synonymous with Chianti, was not planted in Tuscany until the nineteenth century. Which means it's "inconceivable" that we drink the same wine the Sicilian poured the Dread Pirate Roberts during their battle of wits. But if wine is capable of transporting us to a different place and time, then surely Chianti Classico, grown on the dappled hills into which Buttercup and Westley ride into the sunset, will take us to the site of the greatest kiss of all time—as Fezzik will tell you, it was sublime.

Outlander

DIANA GALBALDON

Pairing: Scotch, the older the better

This pairing is plain as day. This first book in Diana Galbaldon's time-traveling Outlander series takes place entirely in Scotland, the vast majority of it in the mid-eighteenth century. The characters sample a wide variety of drinks, but only one lays our scene so well. For those of us unlucky enough to live far from the Highlands, scotch—smoky, peaty, grassy, the essence of the moors—is the perfect thing to take you there. Putting a little research into your selection will reward you here. Although there aren't any Scottish distilleries whose barrels have been filled since the 1740s, there are several dating as far back as the late eighteenth century. (Oban, one of my favorites, first lit their stills in 1794.) The closer you can get in time to Claire, Jaime, and Jonathan, the closer they'll feel as you read. Serve however you like—neat, in a snifter, over a little ice, with a little soda. The characters aren't fussy about how they drink, so I wouldn't be either.

Bridget Jones's Diary

HELEN FIELDING

PAIRING: CHOCOLATINI

Celebrate yourself Bridget Jones style with a chocolatini near at hand when you curl up with this endearing novel of girl power, self-confidence (or lack thereof), and misadventures in love. This drink is silly but charming, a perfect accompaniment to Bridget's viciously comedic lack of social graces or self-esteem. With this drink we're honoring "vodka and Chaka Khan" and Bridget's obsession with chocolate. We're starting on the road to inner poise and authority—paved with cigarettes, calorie counts, and bottles of wine. We're heading to the latest Tarts and Vicars party with bunny tails on and martini glasses in hand, because God knows we're going to need a drink soon.

INGREDIENTS:

1½ ounces vanilla vodka

1 ounce Bailey's Irish Cream

¼ ounce chocolate liqueur (Godiva is a good place to start, but there are many options and you can experiment to find your favorite)

Chocolate shavings for garnish

INSTRUCTIONS:

1. Combine vodka, Bailey's, and chocolate liqueur in a cocktail shaker and top with ice.

2. Shake vigorously for 10–15 seconds and strain into a chilled cocktail glass.

3. Garnish with chocolate shavings.

The Notebook,

NICHOLAS SPARKS

PAIRING: PROVENÇAL ROSÉ

The book that rocketed Nicholas Sparks to international celebrity and eventually became the movie that gifted Ryan Gosling to the world, *The Notebook* is revered by romance lovers the world over. Starring Allie and Noah, lovers young and old, *The Notebook* begins with Noah reading Allie a story about two fiery teenagers who fall in love over a wild summer. Reading this book brings back youthful fantasies about soul mates and true love, and we need a drink for picnics and hot summer days as much as we need one for romance and devotion. Rosé wine hailing from Provence fits both needs. Perhaps the best picnic drink in existence, Provençal rosé is light and airy with crisp, abundant acid. It seems to shout the beauties of blue skies, white clouds, and girls in sundresses. Find a bottle and chill it, pack a blanket and snacks, head into a field, and lie in the summer sun to let Noah and Allie's romance sweep you away.

Carolina Moon

NORA ROBERTS

Pairing: Peach Tea Cocktail

What says Southern more than peaches and sweet tea? How about a big old plantation home surrounded by fields of organic cotton? Or a wealthy landowner who falls in love with the plucky entrepreneur who happens to have paranormal visions? Get in the spirit (pun intended) with a cocktail that'll carry you to those sweltering summer days and seduce you under the cool night moon. Nora Roberts has dozens of published novels, but *Carolina Moon*, a thrilling romance set against the backdrop of a twenty-year-old unsolved murder, is an enduring favorite. You might not plan to fall in love with this zingy, thirst-quenching cocktail, but then, Tory didn't plan to fall in love with Cade Lavelle, either.

INGREDIENTS
2 ounces whiskey or bourbon
½ ounce simple syrup
4 ounces peach-flavored iced tea
Peach slices, for garnish
Lemon wheel, for garnish

INSTRUCTIONS
1. Fill a Collins or highball glass with ice and pour in whiskey and simple syrup.

2. Top with peach iced tea and a few peaches for garnish.

3. Stir well to incorporate and garnish with the lemon wheel.

Note: you can either buy premade peach tea mix or you can make your own. To make your own, make a quart of hot tea with 6–8 bags of black tea such as English breakfast, stir in 2 tablespoon sugar and 2 cups (16 ounce) peach nectar, cover, and chill in the fridge. You can find peach nectar in cans or jars in the juice aisle of the grocery store.

The Time Traveler's Wife

AUDREY NIFFENEGGER

PAIRING: THE CHICAGO

Did you know the Second City, the backdrop for Henry and Claire Abshire's sweet and sensitive romance, has a namesake cocktail? The Chicago cocktail is stiff but elegant, with brandy, Cointreau, and sparkling wine. It originated in the 1890s and was codified in cocktail history when Harry Craddock included it his *Savoy Cocktail Book*. With a deep sweetness and lighthearted enthusiasm, it'll charm you as quickly as Claire charms Henry; still, it's as effervescent as Henry's connection to the present. It pairs as well with an afternoon on a Lincoln Park patio as it does with family breakfast on Christmas day. In short, it's perfect for *The Time Traveler's Wife*. But don't drink too many, lest you, like Henry, develop a bad case of Chrono-Impairment Disorder.

INGREDIENTS:

Lemon wedge
Superfine sugar
1½ ounces brandy
1 dash (approximately ¼ teaspoon) orange liqueur, such as Cointreau, Grand Marnier, or orange curaçao
1–2 dashes Angostura bitters
2–3 ounces champagne (preferably brut)
Lemon twist, for garnish

INSTRUCTIONS

1. Run the lemon wedge around the rim of a chilled cocktail glass, and rim with sugar. (Pour sugar into a small plate, and twist the upside-down glass to coat.)

2. Combine the brandy, orange liqueur, and bitters in a cocktail shaker and top with ice. Stir for 10–15 seconds.

3. Strain into a chilled champagne glass or coupe. Twist the lemon over the glass and set it on top to garnish.

Twilight
STEPHANIE MEYER

PAIRING: WASHINGTON SYRAH

What's an aspiring vampire to do when she can't drink blood yet? Drink red wine from her adoptive home state of Washington, of course. Although Forks, on the Olympic Peninsula, is a far cry from the Washington State wine regions of Walla Walla, the Columbia Valley, or the Yakima Valley, there's no reason not to tie the setting and the theme together with these epic wines from one of America's emergent wine-producing regions. Washington State, like California, is warm enough to fully ripen hardy red grapes, producing massive cabernet sauvignons, Syrahs, cabernet francs, and some excellent red blends, including the southern Rhône style. Of these, the best for this book are the Syrahs or Syrah blends. Juicy and meaty in flavor, smooth and succulent on the palate, these wines are some of Washington's finest and pair beautifully with *Twilight*. I hesitate to say the color is reminiscent of blood, but . . . If you're not yet of wine-drinking age, never fear: Washington also produces the world's widest variety of apples, and given the cover of this book, I'd say one of those (or some apple juice) would make a fine pairing as well.

If I Stay
GAYLE FOREMAN

PAIRING: OREGON PINOT GRIS

If I Stay is neither light nor frivolous, but the tone is gentle, the style youthful and innocent even as it deals with serious issues of life, death, and the most important choice of all. The plot and themes revolve heavily around music—the clash and concord between rock and roll and classical, the Ramones and Beethoven. We need a drink that hails from Oregon, where the book takes place. We also need a drink that matches the wistful innocence of the book. Pinot Gris, a variety that receives both too much censure and too much praise, can be appreciated for what it is when enjoyed without seriousness or great expectations. These wines provide a lyricism and vivacity to complement Mia's narration and her enduring tale of family, loss, and young love.

Water for Elephants

SARA GRUEN

PAIRING: GIN AND GINGER ALE

Many drinks are mentioned in this gem of a tale, from Champagne to moonshine, from high-end brandy to an adulterated ginger extract called "jake," and truthfully any of these drinks will serve. But if you want the real "water for elephants" drink, or at least, the drink an elephant will drain like water, you need gin and ginger ale. As Grzegorz Grabowski, an otherwise irrelevant character, reveals halfway through the book, elephants love alcohol—and Rosie, the star of the Benzini Brothers Most Spectacular Show on Earth, loves gin and ginger ale. This cocktail might not sound romantic, but at least one lady will chase after you with this drink in hand. Don't say I didn't warn you about the big ears and tail.

Fifty Shades of Grey

E. L. JAMES

PAIRING: MERLOT

E. L. James is a wine lover, and she carefully included many different types of wine, both red and white, as props for Anastasia Steele's tumultuous romance with Christian Grey. Our challenge is to come up with a single wine that encapsulates the drama, romance, and seduction of this novel. We need something dark and dangerous, provocative but challenging. It may surprise you to learn that merlot fits the bill perfectly. Not unlike *Fifty Shades of Grey*, merlot has been given a bad rap. It's all Miles Raymond's fault—if he hadn't been so disdainful of merlot in favor of pinot noir, this noble grape would never have fallen by the wayside. But the maligned variety produces one of the most dangerously seductive wines in the world. Merlot is one of nine so-called "noble" varieties originally cultivated in France, and it contributes to some of the finest and most expensive wines in the world, from the Bordeaux region. On its own, merlot is round and supple on the palate, reminiscent of black cherry, chocolate, roses, and dark plum. If that doesn't sound like "tie me up and spank me" to you, then I guess you're just not ready to meet *your* Christian Grey.

The Fault in Our Stars

JOHN GREEN

PAIRING: CHAMPAGNE

Hazel Grace Lancaster and Augustus Waters don't have it easy. As kids suffering from cancer and left out of many of the "normal" things teenagers do, they find salvation in their friends, their families, and each other. But they do have some pretty extraordinary experiences together. From reluctantly falling in love at their cancer support group to traveling together to the Netherlands—even if their trip is coarsely disturbed by the man they were supposed to visit—to sharing a bottle of Champagne at a fancy restaurant in Amsterdam, Hazel and Augustus make a beautiful thing out of a tragic and unfair situation. This book is equal parts young adult novel and romance, so if you're under twenty-one and not lucky enough to be reading in a posh restaurant in Amsterdam, treat yourself to a bottle of sparkling grape juice. Share a bottle of bubbles with these brave young lovers and celebrate the magic found even in terrible times.

BEAUJOLAIS NOUVEAU
CONTEMPORARY LITERARY FICTION

Classic novels that have stood the test of time are, for the most part, written by people who are now dead. But many of our finest works of literature—the books that grace the front tables at our local bookstores—are written by men and women whose works are still evolving. Although a few of these novels were written by artists who are no longer with us, their works feel modern and contemporary. Like Beaujolais nouveau, these books are fresh, vibrant, and sometimes a little weird. They shape how we write today. Reflective of current societal and literary standards, contemporary fiction seeks to make a statement about humanity as we live and breathe. Fortunately, there are stiff drinks to help you wade through such aspirational novels. Read on to find the best drinks to enjoy when your book club picks one of the many daring and ambitious novels of the last century.

One Hundred Years of Solitude

GABRIEL GARCIA MARQUEZ

PAIRING: AGUARDIENTE

Pairing a drink with this immaculate novel proves surprisingly difficult.
What should it be? Though a margarita or a mezcal drink might seem
apropos, both tequila and mezcal come from agave, which is grown in the
deserts of Mexico, not the jungles of Colombia. What about a daiquiri?
Or a mojito? Rum is after all popular in the Caribbean, not far from the
fictional village of Macondo. But a daiquiri is a cosmopolitan cocktail, and
the only time Macondo can be said to be cosmopolitan is in the throes of
exploitation by the banana companies. And a mojito is Cuban by origin—
it would be inopportune to borrow it for a Colombian tale, particularly
when there is an answer, if we know only where to look. *Aguardiente*, a
relatively low-alcohol spirit and a Colombian specialty, is made from native sugar cane and infused with aniseed, and has been popular since the
Spanish ruled. Many South American countries have their own version of
aguardiente—the most famous might be Brazil's *cachaça*—but Colombia is
the only nation to use aniseed as a flavoring agent. Consumed neat, this
spirit is as close to the national drink of Colombia as we can get. It has
a long history in the country—back from before things in the world had
names, and it was necessary to point—and is a long-standing tradition to
take shots with friends. By drinking Colombian *aguardiente*, we are celebrating Garcia Marquez's magical storytelling ability as well as the place
he venerated as home.

Author's note: Can't find aguardiente*? No worries. Fix yourself a quick
margarita for a similar feel with ingredients that can be found at any liquor store in
America.*

INGREDIENTS

Lime slice

Salt

2 ounces silver tequila

1 ounce Cointreau or triple sec

¾ ounce lime juice

INSTRUCTIONS

1. Rub one of the lime slices around the rim of a chilled cocktail glass and rim with salt, reserving the lime slice for garnish. Place glass back in freezer or refrigerator to keep cold.

2. Combine tequila, Cointreau or triple sec, and lime juice in a cocktail shaker. Top up with ice and shake well to mix.

3. Strain into chilled cocktail glass and garnish with the slice of lime.

The Name of the Rose

UMBERTO ECO

PAIRING: TRAPPIST BEER

While you're delving into the labyrinthine scriptorium of Eco's Benedictine monastery, open a bottle of monkish beer. The Trappists, a branch of the Cistercian order, have been brewing beer for centuries as a purer alternative to water, to sell to village-dwellers for a source of income, and to tide them over during the caloric deprivation of the Lenten fast. The Trappist order dates back to the mid-seventeenth century and arose as a reform movement to the corruption of its parent order the Cistercians, whose reform movement, in turn, arose in the early twelve century in response to the degradation of the Benedictines. Fortunately for us, the beer has done the opposite. Trappist beer, centered in Belgium and Germany from the seventeenth century onward, gave rise to the Belgian style of brewing and produces bottles that only improve with age. The best way to experience life alongside William and his protégé Adso is with a high-quality bottle of this deep, contemplative beer. To deepen the pairing, seek out a bottle from an Italian monastery in honor of the book's setting in Piedmont. And to *perfect* the pairing, snag a bottle from Birra Nursia, the only Benedictine abbey in Italy that produces and exports for American consumption.

Blood Meridian

CORMAC MCCARTHY

Pairing: Whiskey

Ten pages into *Blood Meridian*, I was reaching for the shot glass. Never in my life have I read a book that can be so adequately summed up by a simple shot of whiskey. And by that I don't mean to imply, for all you McCarthy diehards, that the book is simple. To do so would be an insult both to whiskey and to McCarthy. Whiskey is woody, earthy, round, sharp, warming, welcoming, and angry, all at the same time. It epitomizes barroom fights, gunshots in a saloon, six-shooter standoffs with tumbleweeds in the background. It's horse thieves, scalping, massacres on the plains. Whiskey is violent and uncivilized. It is, in short, *Blood Meridian*. Whether shooting or sipping, for McCarthy's darkest book—and that's saying something—you'll want a fifth nearby.

The Cider House Rules

JOHN IRVING

PAIRING: HARD APPLE CIDER

Cideries are making a comeback in present-day America, particularly in New England, where this book is set, and there's no better way to experience the world through Homer Wells's eyes than with a crisp glass of apple cider. If it seems a little odd to be drinking alcohol during this Prohibition-era book—well, it is. But as we all know, Prohibition didn't stop anyone, and it shouldn't stop us from enjoying the cider revolution taking place across America right now. And the cider revolution is *happening*. There are single-variety ciders, wild-foraged apples, ciders fermented with different strains of yeast, and so on and so forth. Cideries are beginning to treat cider like wine, and the result is a wonderful proliferation of styles for our enjoyment. To maximize this pairing, find a few bottles from Maine, where this book is set, and taste them over consecutive nights as you settle in to read.

The Handmaid's Tale

MARGARET ATWOOD

PAIRING: THE LIBERATOR

Although it seems paradoxical to drink alcohol while trudging through Atwood's theocratic dystopia, it also feels right: there's pretty much no other way to get through this quiet, dark book than by self-medicating with booze. Because of the time and setting—a near-future world where a theocratic totalitarian government has relegated women to subservient roles as child-bearers and the people live in a state of total deprivation of pleasure—it's hard to choose a wrong pairing. Which is why I chose the Liberator, a cocktail that is a twist on the Communist. Originally conceived in the 1930s as a blend of gin, cherry liqueur, and citrus, the Communist becomes the Liberator with a quick swap of rum for gin. Drain one or two of these and toast to our social, political, and sexual freedoms. This book will definitely make you appreciate them.

INGREDIENTS
1¼ ounces white rum
3 ounces cherry liqueur
½ ounce lemon juice
½ ounce orange juice
¼ ounce simple syrup
Maraschino cherry, for garnish

INSTRUCTIONS
1. Combine all ingredients (except the cherry) in a cocktail shaker over ice and shake well to mix.

2. Strain over ice and garnish with the cherry.

Strong Motion,

JONATHAN FRANZEN

PAIRING: SPARKLING WINE

There's an undercurrent of joyous enthusiasm running through this book. You turn the pages, welcomed and convinced that there is a redemption story coming eventually, or at least that the bad guys will get their just deserts. The fact that the book begins with a funeral and ends with a series of weddings and engagements—the classic rom-com formula—contributes to the sense that the book is only negative about the human condition in the short term. In the long term, everything will be all right. Which is why the pairing for this book is sparkling wine. This might seem a strange choice. But there's nothing else that represents a celebration like a glass of bubbles—and nor is there any other drink that so well sums up the lifestyles of the rich and famous. With free-market, unregulated American capitalism in Franzen's crosshairs, combined with his stylistic penchant for levity and brightness, a succulent bottle of American bubbles is your best bet as a challenging but lively pairing for this modern classic.

The Secret History

DONNA TARTT

Pairing: Vin Jaune

To the intellectually elitist, aesthete students of Julian Morrow, *vin jaune* might not be quite up to snuff. It is not regarded as one of the finest wines in the world, nor is it currently particularly famous. But our students defile their abstractions of beauty and knowledge with murder, lies, and betrayal, so we should not fear to "stoop" so low as to enjoy a drink not up to their standards. Elitism aside, *vin jaune* is wonderful—voluptuous but incisive, warm but bright. French for "yellow wine," this is an un-fortified wine hailing from the Jura region in Eastern France (wedged between Burgundy on its western side and Geneva to the east) with sim-ilar flavor and texture characteristics as sherry. Tartt's prose in this novel is yellow-edged with deceit; it seems everyone is lying, just slightly, about something. Behind the love of beauty and intellectual power is a monster, lurking in the dark. Something is always hidden. The cards never laid on the table. So too with *vin jaune*—it never stops opening, never stops changing. The secrets in the glass are never fully revealed.

Infinite Jest,

DAVID FOSTER WALLACE

PAIRING: AMERICAN PINOT NOIR

All of *Infinite Jest* is an argument against addiction. Some of the book's most impactful scenes take place at weekly meetings of a Boston chapter of Alcoholics Anonymous, which is why whatever we pair with this book must be carefully chosen to walk the line between enjoyment and dependence. For this reason, we should studiously avoid anything with hard alcohol in it—the dangers are too clear. Besides, I have difficulty imagining a cocktail that could capture the vastness of this work: the immense undertaking of writing it, the give-and-take between intellectual achievement and self-flagellation, or the existential angst crossbred with morbid humor throughout. But there is a drink that strikes the balance we seek. Devotees of pinot noir (like David Foster Wallace's most ardent fans) will tell you there's nothing like it in the world. The finest examples strike a careful balance between structure and flow, brightness and depth, poise and exuberance—the same balance David Foster Wallace weaves through his magnum opus. Pinot noir is sophisticated enough to match the book's polymath intellectualism, deep enough for its moments of tragedy, and light enough in body and spirit to match the book's levity and quick-witted genius. If you are going to drink alcohol with this book, pinot noir is the way to go. Why American? Because *Infinite Jest* is a decidedly American book, dealing with problems, systems, and character tropes specific to America (and, to some extent, Canada). This book is so long, it may take you months to read, so spend that time experimenting to find your favorite styles. Taste wines from the Willamette Valley to the Sonoma Coast and all the way down south to the Santa Ynez Valley. By the end, you'll have learned a whole lot—about yourself, about pinot noir, and about one of modern literature's crowning achievements from a writer who was taken from us too soon.

Fight Club

CHUCK PALAHNIUK

PAIRING: LAGER, BY THE PITCHER, FROM YOUR LOCAL DIVE

Picture in your mind the bar where a fight club is taking place in the basement. What's it look like? There's a veneer of grease on the tables and counters. Right? There's a bartender in a white tank top, hoop earrings, and bad makeup. Right? The lighting is shit, and not because there are candles at every table or Edison bulbs in the fixtures. It smells like old smoke with an overlay of body odor. There's a guy lighting a cigarette out front. Right? This is the kind of bar where a fight club is held. And are you drinking craft beer here? Are you drinking craft cocktails here? No, you are not. You're sharing a pitcher of Bud Light. Or High Life. Or PBR. If you're lucky, there's a tap of Sierra Nevada Pale Ale on offer. If you're really lucky, you'll get a cheap maraschino cherry in your Jack and coke when you wink at the bartender. This is *Fight Club*. Not some Manhattan social club. And Jack is not getting a "chardonnay barrel-aged Belgian-style sour" at this bar, no matter how broken his heart may be.

The Red Tent

ANITA DIAMANT

PAIRING: LEVANTINE BEER

In the early days of civilization, beer was the most common alcohol around. Although the first mention of alcohol in the Bible is wine ("Noah, a man of the soil, proceeded to plant a vineyard"), Diamant's retelling of the story of Dinah and the family of Jacob primarily (and accurately) references beer. Making beer was women's work. While the men worked in the fields, farming and herding, the women stayed at home to perfect their food and their brews. In *The Red Tent*, the women are frequently engaged in brewing, and they present offerings of beer at social and ceremonial events. Later, working in Egypt, Dinah would have been surrounded by beer, where the cities were saturated with the stuff. Beer was rationed out as a meal for laborers, paid as a wage to craftsmen and farmers, or doled out in massive quantities at royal feasts or as a bride-price. And although it might not be possible to get your hands on a true Egyptian or Mesopotamian beer quite like the ones Dinah and her family would have enjoyed, you can enjoy a diverse selection of modern craft beers from the Levant with them in spirit. Because of the Islamic tradition of abstaining from alcohol, breweries in the modern-day land of Canaan are few and far between. But there are Israeli and Lebanese brewers infused with the spirit of the craft beer revolution. Find what you can, buy a six-pack (or several), and serve this unique brew when you sit down to discuss Diamant's powerful retelling of an ancient tale.

Underworld

DON DELILLO

PAIRING: LONG ISLAND ICED TEA

There are two possible approaches to this novel. The first is to pour yourself a shot of vodka. As the purest distilled spirit, vodka is the best representation of one aspect of DeLillo's ambitious novel: to find a common thread that represents and connects all systems, all humans, all experiences in America during the Cold War. To distill the massive interconnectedness of all things down to a singular object—in this case, a single baseball. The second approach is to take that shot of vodka and throw it into a messy and over-the-top but delicious cocktail that, instead of distilling to the basics, seeks to depict the totality, the monstrosity. I prefer this approach. Have you seen the size of this book? If DeLillo knew anything about distilling, it would weigh about a pound less. A Long Island Iced Tea, renowned as the booziest cocktail money can buy, combines vodka, rum, whiskey, tequila, triple sec, lemon juice, simple syrup, and cola in equal proportions and miraculously results in something that tastes good. If that's not the ideal representation of DeLillo's *Underworld*, I don't know what is.

INGREDIENTS

¾ ounce gin
¾ ounce white rum
¾ ounce silver tequila
¾ ounce vodka
¾ ounce triple sec
¾ ounce simple syrup
¾ ounce lemon juice
Cola
Lemon wedge, for garnish

INSTRUCTIONS

1. Fill a highball or a Collins glass with ice and add all ingredients except the cola.

2. Top with a splash of cola and stir briefly to mix. Garnish with the lemon wedge.

The Poisonwood Bible

BARBARA KINGSOLVER

PAIRING: TAP WATER

What would a group of Baptists drink on an evangelical mission to the Belgian Congo? Definitely not alcohol. As a stridently religious family transplanted unprepared into the otherworldly jungle of the Congo, you can bet these folks aren't sitting around drinking booze. Nor are the villagers of Kilanga, where these naïve Americans set up their mission. And since the modern-day Democratic Republic of the Congo is in a severe water crisis wherein less than half the population has access to clean drinking water—a direct and indirect result of the colonizing influence of white colonizers like the Price family—there's no better way to appreciate the complicated history of this region and the impact of evangelization and colonization than by walking to your kitchen sink and opening the tap. Pour yourself a glass of water and remember that this is a privilege not everyone in the world is lucky enough to enjoy.

Life of Pi

YANN MARTEL

PAIRING: BENGALI TIGER

When I was six months out of college and wet behind the ears in the world of booze, I talked my way into a serving job at a restaurant in Chicago called Veerasway. (Or they took pity on me. Either way.) The restaurant has since closed, but this job was my first introduction to the world of cocktails. From a Pimm's Cup to a "Veeralassi" (a dessert-style mango lassi with coconut-infused rum) to a Ginger-Cucumber Fizz, we had an amazing array of Indian-flavored cocktails that everyone seemed to love. But the most popular drink we served—and certainly the most intriguing—was a drink called the Bengali Tiger. Years later, while reading *Life of Pi* for the first time, my mind flew to this cocktail. It's an evocative drink: sweet from the exotic fruit flavors of tamarind, date, and pineapple, but balanced with a spice blend of green and black cardamom and a sprinkling of ghost chili powder. This was the real deal. It was even a burnt-orange color, evocative of a tiger's bright stripes. This cocktail requires a time investment to make, but it's well worth the effort, especially if you're going to spend the next several days reading about a man stuck on board a life raft with a Bengal tiger. At least we're consuming the tiger and not the other way around.

(continued on page 145)

INGREDIENTS FOR VANILLA BEAN–INFUSED VODKA
(THIS NEEDS TO BE MADE AT LEAST 4–5 DAYS IN ADVANCE)
750 mL unflavored vodka
1 large vanilla bean

INSTRUCTIONS
1. Slice the vanilla bean from stem to stern, leaving it attached slightly at the top so it takes the shape of a V.

2. Fill a large quart jar or an empty (clean) vodka bottle with vodka and drop in the vanilla bean.

3. Set in a cool, dark place to infuse, and shake a few times a day to mix and integrate the flavors.

4. Taste daily, and when the vanilla flavor is strong enough for you to taste clearly, strain out the vanilla bean using a mesh sieve and a funnel into a second clean glass jar for storage. Label clearly so you don't forget what's inside!

INGREDIENTS FOR THE TAMARIND-DATE PUREE (MAKES ABOUT 2 CUPS)
½ cup tamarind paste
½ cup dates, pitted
2¼ cups water
½ cup jaggery or brown sugar
¾ teaspoon green cardamom
¾ teaspoon black cardamom (for both green and black cardamom, it's ideal to buy cardamom pods and grind in a spice grinder just prior to using, but buying ground spices works as well if whole pods are not available)

INSTRUCTIONS
1. Combine tamarind paste, dates, and water in a saucepan and bring to a boil. Reduce heat to a simmer and cook, stirring occasionally, until dates are soft, 8–10 minutes.

2. Add jaggery or brown sugar and stir until the sugar has dissolved and the mixture starts to thicken.

(continued on page 146)

3. Add both ground cardamoms and remove from heat, stirring to combine.

4. Let cool several minutes and transfer to a blender. Blend until smooth, adding a little additional water if necessary. The mixture should be like a creamy soup in viscosity—you should be able to pour it without trouble from a jar or storage vessel. Remember that it will thicken as it cools, so a little thinner is better now.

5. Strain using a fine mesh sieve to remove any chunks of fruit. Transfer to a glass jar to cool and store.

INGREDIENTS FOR THE COCKTAIL

2 ounces vanilla bean–infused vodka (make at home for best results—see above—or buy vanilla-flavored vodka)

¾ ounce tamarind-date puree (recipe above)

¼ ounce pineapple juice (store-bought works fine here)

Spicy ground chili powder (cayenne or, if you're feeling adventurous, ghost), for garnish

INSTRUCTIONS

1. In a cocktail shaker, combine vodka, tamarind-date puree, and pineapple juice. Top with ice and shake very well, 15–20 seconds, to combine.

2. Strain into a chilled cocktail glass and sprinkle with chili powder to garnish.

The Kite Runner

KHALED HOSSEINI

PAIRING: ARABIC COFFEE

Arabic coffee is known by many names. The most famous is Turkish coffee, but what you call it depends on where you are. If you're in Cypress, it's a Cypriot coffee. If you're in Greece, it's a Greek coffee. If you're in Turkey, it's a Turkish coffee. And so on. By and large, they're all prepared the same way, and they share an origin story: The Ottoman Sultan Suleiman the Magnificent was introduced to the beverage by one of his governors from Yemen. The Magnificent Sultan fell in love with this drink (who wouldn't?) and it quickly became popular in Istanbul and throughout the Ottoman Empire. Now, Arabic coffee by any name is a particular hallmark of regions where alcohol is banned for religious reasons, such as Afghanistan, where *The Kite Runner* takes place. Cardamom is ground alongside the roasted beans, and the ground coffee and cardamom are brewed together in a *dallah*, a traditional metal kettle designed to extract more from the beans and aerate the coffee to generate more foam. This creamy, spicy beverage instantly transports the drinker to a place that looks and smells like young Amir's Kabul, full of mud houses, flowering courtyards, bright mosaics, and the imams' calls to prayer.

The Namesake

JHUMPA LAHIRI

PAIRING: MASALA SOUR

This book exists at the curious intersection of Indian and American culture with a sharp overlay of Russian literature. The story begins with a decisively Indian narrative: a young Bengali couple move to Massachusetts together, so the husband, Ashoke, can get his engineering doctorate at MIT. His wife Ashima is soon pregnant with their first child, who is named Gogol after the Russian writer Nikolai Gogol and eventually becomes the central focus of the narrative as he struggles through the challenges and complexities of life as a second-generation immigrant. The cocktail, created by New Delhi mixologist Topesh Chatterjee, fuses all three cultures in one cocktail: modeled on a traditional sour (American) with Indian flavors and Russia's most famous beverage as the spirit base.

INGREDIENTS
1 bag masala (chai) tea
2 ounces vodka
1 egg white
¾ ounce lemon juice
¾ ounce simple syrup
Orange slice, for garnish
Cinnamon stick, for garnish

INSTRUCTIONS
1. Combine all but the orange slice and cinnamon in a cocktail shaker. If the tea bag has a string, cut it off at the base of the bag. Top with ice and shake well, 10–15 seconds.

2. Strain into a chilled coupe or cocktail glass and garnish with the orange slice and the cinnamon stick.

Snow Flower and the Secret Fan

LISA SEE

PAIRING: BAIJIU

A masterful telling of an achingly beautiful tale, *Snow Flower and the Secret Fan* is both painful to read and impossible to put down. *Baijiu*, a distilled spirit high in alcohol, has been an intrinsic part of Chinese culture for centuries. The first still used for alcoholic purposes was likely imported from Arabia, where distillation was invented, and the earliest known still in China has been dated approximately to the twelfth century. Clear distilled spirits are historically popular in China, and would have been common during the nineteenth century, when Lily and Snow Flower were writing their secrets onto their fan. Indeed, *baijiu* is commonly served at weddings, celebrations, business meetings, and other social gatherings, particularly as a traditional toast shared by all attendants. You'll want something emblematic of all the beauty and pain Lily and Snow Flower experience throughout their quietly passionate lives—and that's what you'll get with this fierce and unapproachable drink, which is both hard to swallow and worth the pain. Sound familiar? If not, it will once you're finished with the book. *Baijiu* is accessible in America, though you may have to call around for it—it's not the most popular drink in this country. Once you've found a bottle, adorn a small, chilled glass with edible flowers to make the pairing complete.

The Brief Wondrous Life of Oscar Wao

JUNOT DÍAZ

PAIRING: MAMAJUANA

This was a tricky one. Díaz's wondrous story alternates between New Jersey and the Dominican Republic as Oscar, the titular hero, his sister Lola, and the narrator Yunior navigate the murky waters of adolescence, sexuality, immigration, and racial divisions. What ought to be the pairing? A hybrid of the two cultures, like a Corn and Oil, a margarita, or a Mojito? These are all rum-based drinks, popular in the United States, and would have integrated the two narratives well. Or should we go with a truly Dominican drink like *mamajuana*, a rum-based infusion of native herbs and spices hailing from the Dominican Republic itself? Ultimately, it was the *fukú*, a curse placed on the New World the day the Europeans arrived on Hispaniola as conquerors and ravagers and one of the book's running themes, that convinced me it had to be *mamajuana*. (But a Corn and Oil is a particularly good backup if your liquor store doesn't stock *mamajuana*.) After all, both the *fukú* and *mamajuana* are very old—it is thought that the *mamajuana* herbal blend could be as old as eight hundred years, while the *fukú*, the curse that defines Oscar Wao's brief life (and the lives of so many Antilles) originated with the landfall of Christopher Columbus. Get your hands on a bottle of this unique spirit if you can, and whisper *zafa* periodically as you read to keep the *fukú* at bay.

Author's note: mamajuana is almost as hard to find as Colombian aguardiente *(page 130), so if you can't get your hands on this special liquor, try a Corn and Oil cocktail instead.*

INGREDIENTS

2 ounces blackstrap or aged Barbados rum

½ ounce falernum

½ ounce fresh lime juice

4 dashes Angostura bitters

Lime wedge, for garnish

INSTRUCTIONS

1. In a rocks or an Old Fashioned glass, combine rum, falernum, and lime juice, and top up with crushed ice.

2. Add 3 dashes Angostura bitters on top and stir well to combine, 10–15 seconds.

3. Garnish with 1 more dash of bitters and the lime wedge.

1Q84
HARUKI MURAKAMI

PAIRING: SCOTCH WHISKEY

You thought I was going to say sake, didn't you? Sake is the national drink of Japan. Why wouldn't you drink sake while reading a book from one of the living masters of literature—who happens to be from Japan? Well, you thought wrong. The young, hip, postmodern folks in Japan aren't drinking sake. The young, hip, postmodern folks in Japan like Aomame and Tengo are drinking beer, cocktails, gin, whiskey, or, best of all, scotch. And since *1Q84* encapsulates so many intricacies of modern Japanese culture, you don't want to get mired in the past. What you need is good scotch whiskey. Cutty Sark is mentioned in the novel, though it's best not to be too discerning—lest you become "sexually bland" in Aomame's words—and besides, there are plenty of other good scotches out there on the market. The book is long. A glass or two of scotch per reading session will put you to bed in no time. I recommend taking advantage of this opportunity to experiment and find your scotch preferences. Pour yourself a glass, on the rocks, just in time to climb down the emergency escape ladder and slip into this subtle and bizarre dystopian world.

CAN I SEE YOUR I.D.?
JUNIOR PAIRINGS FOR YOUNG ADULT BOOKS

While I don't condone the consumption of alcoholic beverages by minors, this is primarily because my lawyer told me not to. Besides, we all know young adult books aren't just for young adults. Kids, adults, grandparents, dogs, cats, and Ghosts of Christmases Past can all enjoy young adult books just as much as teens—you just have to get in touch with that moody, hormonal side from your teenage years. These pairings are mostly nonalcoholic, but if you're of age and a fan of young adult novels, many can easily be made boozy. There are tips and suggestions in the descriptions and recipes.

The Call of the Wild

JACK LONDON

PAIRING: SNOW

In 2016, NPR's *The Salt* did an investigation into the rumors that snow is not safe to eat. I was emotionally invested in the outcome of this investigation. Some of my fondest childhood memories involve chowing down on a bowl of snow mixed with honey after a big winter storm. *The Salt* concluded that the rumors of snow being unsafe to eat are not entirely without merit—snow does pick up particulates out of the atmosphere, especially in the early hours of a storm. But after the first few hours, those particulates have precipitated out, and by and large the levels of any threatening or harmful chemicals in snow are orders of magnitude less concentrated than what is recommended for safe drinking water. This does not mean it's always safe to eat snow, but nor does it mean you shouldn't. This is convenient, because snow is a great pairing for *The Call of the Wild*. Snow is obviously connected to the Yukon territories, and, although eating snow in an Alaskan winter might give you hypothermia, it's a great way to evoke the setting from the lower forty-eight. If you can't get snow—because it's summer, or because of some other pesky detail like "I live in Florida"—or you happen to be a particularly health-conscious parent determined to avoid all chemicals, a snow cone will do just as well. (Truthfully, I'm not sure the substances in those sno-cone syrups are any better for your kids than snow.) Mix your snow with a little honey or sugar and eat up, dreaming of Buck and his transformation into the one of wild wolves of Alaska.

Johnny Tremain
ESTHER FORBES

PAIRING: COFFEE

Take it however you like: with cream and sugar, or just cream, or just sugar, or as black as your soul. A simple cup of coffee not only celebrates the American revolutionaries' resistance to "taxation without representation" and the infamous Boston Tea Party, it also features prominently in young Johnny's experience when, his pockets rich with silver, he goes to fill his belly at a local tavern and orders coffee for the first time. He's long been entranced with the warm, earthy smell, but when he drinks the stuff, he finds it disappointingly bitter. Sip a cup of this strong, bitter brew as you read Forbes's powerful story about a young man swept up in the forces of history.

A Tree Grows in Brooklyn

BETTY SMITH

PAIRING: CHICORY COFFEE

While twenty-first-century Williamsburg gentrifies as New York City grows ever wealthier, Francie Nolan's impoverished twentieth-century Irish family makes do with the square end of the cow's tongue, wilted carrots and celery, and chicory root in their coffee to make it taste stronger. Her mother knows a dozen different ways to use stale bread—most of which include ketchup—and Francie lets the junk man pinch her cheeks for an extra penny when she and her brother sell the week's collection of trash. But all told, the Nolans are as happy as can be expected. More than anything, this book is about being determined, scrappy, and making the best out of what you've got. Nowhere is this more evident than in the joy and delight the Nolans get from what food they have. Sipping a steaming cup of chicory coffee while you curl up with this book will bring home the sacrifices made and small delights found by Francie and her persevering family.

Lord of the Flies

WILLIAM GOLDING

PAIRING: COCONUT WATER

Did the boys eat coconuts on their jungle island in the middle of the ocean as they murdered each other one by one? Does it matter if they did or didn't? Coconut water sings of the hot sun, fruit trees ripe for the picking, dense leafy underbrush, and sandy beaches with cracked, bloody skulls on them. Wait. Did I say that last part out loud? Whatever the brutal events of this book, coconut water will transport you to the schoolboys' idyllic island and give a bit of sweet relief from the violence Golding believes is intrinsic to mankind.

A Wrinkle in Time

MADELINE L'ENGLE

PAIRING: TEA-ZERAC

Get it? Like if you combine *tesseract, Sazerac* and *tea*? Whether or not my pun skills got you wrinkled enough to laugh, this cocktail is weird enough to go with L'Engle's classic sci-fi novel. This cocktail is a simplified version of—you guessed it—a Sazerac, replacing the earthy, woody flavors of rye whiskey with cooled rooibos tea. (Not sure what rooibos is? Flip to the pairing for *The Lorax* on page 192.) This "mocktail" feels enough like a real cocktail that your kids won't feel left out when you head for a nightcap. You won't get a buzz drinking this lovely nonalcoholic cocktail, but it is relaxing enough to put the kids to sleep instead of staying up all night to find out how Meg rescues Charles Wallace from IT.

INGREDIENTS (MAKES ENOUGH TEA FOR 4 DRINKS)
8–10 ounces water
1½ tablespoons dried rooibos tea
4 teaspoons sugar
Peychaud's bitters
Angostura bitters

INSTRUCTIONS (FOR 1 DRINK)
1. Place cocktail glasses in the freezer to chill.

2. Fill a tea ball with rooibos tea leaves. Bring water to a boil, then pour over rooibos tea in a mug and leave to steep for 5 minutes.

3. Once steeped, set the mug in an ice bath to cool (if preparing the drinks immediately) or set aside to cool until room temperature.

4. In a cocktail shaker, muddle together 1 teaspoon sugar, 3 dashes Peychaud's bitters, and 2 dashes Angostura bitters.

5. Top with 2 ounces cooled rooibos tea and a generous serving of ice. Stir for 10–15 seconds and strain into a chilled cocktail glass.

Go Ask, Alice

BEATRICE SPARKS

PAIRING: KOMBUCHA

Kombucha might seem a strange pairing for one of the darkest books in the history of literature, but we need something healthful and uplifting to resuscitate our spirits after such a life-draining book. *Go Ask Alice* has shocked readers young and old since it was published with its portrayal of sexuality, abuse, and drug use and addiction. You'll want something soothing and revitalizing while reading about the narrator's devastating experiences with heroin, LSD, prostitution, and child abuse. Kombucha is nowhere near as addictive as the substances in the book, but its tonic of vinegar, tea, and sweetness provide a happier alternative. And while its health benefits may not be scientifically proven, it is certainly a better option than the lifestyle portrayed in Sparks's narrative. Use a bottle of this nourishing probiotic to nurse you through this bitter story.

The Blue Sword

ROBIN MCKINLEY

PAIRING: DOUGH

No—not dough as in bread dough. *Dough*, or *doogh*, is a salted yogurt drink similar to a lassi but with mint and cucumber instead. Although the province of Damar in the country of Daria is fictional, McKinley loosely based the Hillfolk on the people of Afghanistan, and Daria on India. The Damarians, with their reverence for horses, are sure to drink fermented horse milk at celebrations, and probably incorporate a good amount of horse milk, yogurt, and cheese into their daily meals. *Dough*, a fresh, crisp Persian-Afghani specialty that can be easily made with ingredients at home, will help cool you down after a long, hot day of riding and sword-fighting in this dreamy desert world—even if we have to make do with cow or goat yogurt instead.

INGREDIENTS [SERVES 4]
3½ cups full-fat yogurt
2 cups water
2 cups crushed or small cubes ice
2 Persian cucumbers, roughly chopped
10–12 mint leaves, roughly chopped,
   plus 4 mint sprigs for garnish
¼ teaspoon kosher salt
¼ teaspoon black salt

INSTRUCTIONS
1. In a blender, process all ingredients except the mint sprigs set aside for garnish. Blend until smooth.

2. Serve in chilled glasses. Garnish each glass with fresh mint.

Note: Dough is traditionally thinner than lassi, more like a whole milk than a milkshake. If you're looking for a lassi-like consistency, you will want to reduce the water to ½–1 cup and blend slowly to your desired consistency.

Redwall

BRIAN JACQUES

PAIRING: STRAWBERRY CORDIAL

Brian Jacques clearly had a deep appreciation for the finer things in life—food, friends, and celebrations. The *Redwall* books feature monumental feasts and celebrations, the likes of which can be difficult to imagine for modern readers accustomed to smaller gatherings far removed from great, torchlit halls. Strawberry cordial, also known as strawberry fizz, is one of the most popular beverages with the Redwallers, and it conveniently makes a delicious nonalcoholic drink that's easily adapted into a patio-ready cocktail. Whip up a pitcher of strawberry cordial for the young'uns and pour some sparkling wine on top for yourself, and soon enough you'll all be munching rich bread and cheese, burning your tongue on hotroot soup, and mowing through sweet damson pies—all while valiantly fighting to preserve the Abbey from the vermin beyond the walls.

(continued on page 162)

INGREDIENTS (MAKES ABOUT 1.5 LITERS)
1 pound crushed fresh strawberries
1 lemon, halved and thinly sliced
2 pounds superfine sugar
¼ cup fresh-squeezed lemon juice
2 cups water
Sparkling wine such as *cava* or prosecco
Whole fresh strawberries, for garnish (optional)
Mint sprigs, for garnish (optional)

INSTRUCTIONS:
1. Place the strawberries and the lemon in a large glass bowl along with the lemon juice and sugar.

2. Bring the water to a boil. When it has reached boiling, pour it into the bowl with the strawberries and sugar and mix until the sugar is dissolved.

3. Cover and leave to cool. Refrigerate for 4–6 days, depending on the desired strength of your infusion.

4. Strain through cheesecloth and transfer either to a large pitcher for serving immediately or to sterilized jars. Cordial will keep for up to 4 months in the refrigerator.

5. Serve either over ice with sparkling water (for the kids) or in a champagne glass topped with sparkling wine (for you). Garnish with one or two fresh strawberries and a sprig of mint.

The Giver
LOIS LOWRY

Pairing: Orange Juice

In a book about the giving and receiving of communal memory, what could be better than a drink that nostalgically recalls shared family breakfasts? As a kid, weekend breakfasts were the best thing ever. My dad would make French toast (the best in the world), we'd slice up bananas and strawberries, smother our plates in maple syrup, and drink OJ by the quart. As an adult, not much makes me happier than sharing stacks of pancakes with friends and family over a pitcher of mimosas. In *The Giver*, Jonas spends a lot of time around the table with his family, sharing memories, emotions, and dreams. But when Jonas meets the Giver, the old man opens his eyes to a whole world of new experiences. Pour a big glass of orange juice (and add bubbles if you're of age), share a meal with Jonas and his family, and watch him awaken to the vast swath of human experience through the Giver's memories.

Parable of the Sower

OCTAVIA E. BUTLER

PAIRING: POMEGRANATE SPRITZER

Octavia Butler's eloquent tale of an America torn apart by massive inequality, corporate greed, and global warming hits a little too close to home these days. To appreciate the pains and perils Lauren Oya Olamina must endure in her quest for self-preservation, let's enjoy a drink that resonates with two overarching themes in the book: seeds and water. Pomegranates, native to Iran and northern India and grown in warm, dry areas of the world, will likely flourish in a changing climate—but only to a point. The title, *Parable of the Sower*, comes from one of Jesus's parables in the New Testament, and since some historians argue that the fruit Eve ate from the tree of knowledge was more likely a pomegranate than an apple, we're keeping with the biblical theme as well. A pomegranate spritzer, served with soda water for the teens (and vodka and soda for the adults), allows us to enjoy a hydrating drink laden with seeds to nourish the future of our Earth.

INGREDIENTS

4 ounces pomegranate juice (store-bought or homemade; to make enough for several drinks: seed 4 pomegranates and discard the white pulp; puree the seeds and strain through a fine mesh strainer)
½ ounce lime juice
1 ounce simple syrup
2 ounces vodka (if using)
4 ounces soda water
Pomegranate seeds, for garnish (optional)
Lime wedge, for garnish (optional)
Hibiscus flower, for garnish (optional)

INSTRUCTIONS

1. Combine the pomegranate juice, lime juice, simple syrup, and vodka (if using) in a cocktail shaker and top with ice. Shake for 10–15 seconds.

2. Strain into a glass filled with ice and top with soda water. Garnish with pomegranate, lime, and hibiscus flower.

Sabriel

GARTH NIX

PAIRING: ROOT BEER

Although there is a perfect adult beverage for this pairing called the Necromancer (a variation on the Corpse Reviver with considerably more absinthe), root beer, as dark and cold as the necromancy of the Abhorsens, is a perfectly valid nonalcoholic pairing. Root beer, with all its woody, earthy flavors of birch and sassafras, evokes the decomposition of death, but with a brightness that speaks of the vivacity and energy of magic. Pour an ice-cold mug as you float along the river of death, fly with the Paperwings, and use the bandolier of bells to bind and unbind the black spirits of the dead.

Harry Potter and the Sorcerer's Stone

J. K. ROWLING

PAIRING: BUTTERBEER

If you're reading any of the Harry Potter books, whether you're joining Hagrid in the Leaky Cauldron for the first time or seeking out the Horcruxes scattered across the world, you're going to want some butterbeer. Yes, I know that butterbeer doesn't actually show up until *Harry Potter and The Prisoner of Azkaban*, but let's be honest: it's the most memorable drink from the series (except maybe Polyjuice Potion, and I wouldn't wish that on anyone). Sweet, warming, and mildly alcoholic (in the books—our version is virgin), butterbeer serves as a communal beverage and a relaxing treat. If you, like me, desperately wish you were born not a Muggle but a witch or a wizard, butterbeer is the closest we can come to pretending. In the days after the Universal Studios' Wizarding World opened, their butterbeer recipe was the subject of much discussion. The Associated Press published a recipe that is widely believed to be very similar to the one served at the Leaky Cauldron at Universal Studios. Get your broomstick and wand and knock back a mug of this creamy drink, because there are dark things coming your way, and you'll need your wits about you.

INGREDIENTS (MAKES 4 SERVINGS)

1 cup brown sugar
2 tablespoons water
6 tablespoons butter
½ teaspoon salt
½ teaspoon apple cider vinegar
¾ cup heavy whipping cream, divided
½ teaspoon rum extract
4 (12-ounce) bottles cream
   soda

INSTRUCTIONS

1. In a small saucepan, over medium heat, combine the water and brown sugar and bring to a boil. Stir often until the mixture reads 240°F on a candy thermometer.

2. Remove from heat and promptly stir in butter, salt, cider vinegar, and ¼ cup whipping cream. When fully incorporated, set aside to cool.

3. When mixture has cooled, stir in the rum extract.

4. Combine 2 tablespoon of the brown sugar mixture and the remainder of the heavy cream in a medium mixing bowl. Using an electric mixer or a stand mixer, beat the heavy cream until just thickened, but not completely whipped. This should take 2–3 minutes.

5. To serve, divide the sugar mixture between 4 tall, chilled glasses. Add ¼ cup of cream soda and stir to combine. Top with the remainder of the cream soda and spoon the cream over the top.

Holes

LOUIS SACHAR

PAIRING: SPLOOSH (BELLINI)

Is it possible to combine peaches and onions in a concoction that will simultaneously nourish you in the desert of Green Lake and repel poisonous spotted lizards? Probably—but the mixologist who dares to climb that mountain must be braver than I. A Bellini, evocative of the "sploosh" Zero discovers while hiding under a desiccated canoe, will do just fine until then. (If you'd like, you can caramelize some of Sam's sweet onions as a garnish, but that seems more appropriate for a Bloody Mary than a Bellini.) Although traditionally white peach purée is used for the base of a Bellini, we'll use the ripest, yellowest peaches we can find, in honor of Katherine Barlow's famous spiced peaches. Soon you'll all be strong enough to climb God's thumb, where the water is clean, the onions are sweet, and curses are broken.

INGREDIENTS

2–3 fresh yellow peaches, peeled, pitted, cut into slices, and puréed, plus
   extra slices for garnish
4–6 ounces chilled sparkling wine such as *cava* or prosecco or nonalcoholic
   sparkling grape juice
Ground clove, for garnish

INSTRUCTIONS

1. Pour 3 ounces peach purée into a white wine glass. Pour in the
    sparkling wine or grape juice slowly, stirring gently as you do, so as
    not to lose too much carbonation.

2. Drop a peach slice into the glass for garnish and dust the surface of
    the drink with a sprinkling of ground clove.

The Perks of Being a Wallflower

STEPHEN CHBOSKY

PAIRING: WHATEVER FIRST GOT YOU DRUNK IN HIGH SCHOOL (AND IF YOU'RE STILL IN HIGH SCHOOL, MY LAWYER HAS TOLD ME I CAN'T LEGALLY RECOMMEND ALCOHOLIC BEVERAGES TO YOU, BUT SHE DIDN'T SAY ANYTHING ABOUT TELLING YOU WHAT **NOT** TO DRINK, SO I WILL ADVISE YOU NOW THAT WARM GIN STOLEN FROM YOUR PARENTS' LIQUOR CABINET IS NOT A GOOD PLACE TO START).

There's a lot of experimentation in this book. At the beginning, Charlie is so innocent he doesn't know what masturbation is. By the end, he's experimented with sex, marijuana, alcohol, LSD, social interaction, literature, and writing his own stories. (It's a wonder Chbosky managed to pack so much novelty into such a small package.) If you're currently in high school, chances are you're already experimenting with at least one of these things (don't worry, I won't tell your parents) and you don't need to be transported back into that world. But for the rest of us, the pairing for this book should be deeply personal: it should be whatever takes you back to those high school days when every experience was fresh, strange, and new. Do whatever you need to do—put on that record you were obsessed with in high school, smoke an irregularly shaped joint, buy a twelve-pack of watery beer, or just drive around with the volume up and the windows down—immersing yourself in Chbosky's book involves leaping back into your own disjointed, hopeful shoes.

Speak

LAURIE HALSE ANDERSON

PAIRING: CHOCOLATE-AVOCADO SMOOTHIE

Like *Go Ask Alice*, Laurie Halse Anderson's bitingly funny, cynical yet optimistic novel demands a healing beverage. Melinda's internal monologue slowly reveals a dark story of rape and post-traumatic stress disorder, and the accompanying experience of being an outcast in high school. Trees are critical to Melinda's healing process, as she draws herself a forest of trees in which to hide her trauma from prying eyes while she recovers, and also allows herself to grow from seed. With this smoothie, we're honoring two of the most important trees in present-day Western food culture: the avocado and the cacao. Both are massive rainforest plants, with generous shelter and life-giving fruits that will heal us on our individual journeys to recovery from trauma. Let this delicious smoothie, as well as Melinda's strength and growth, nourish and nurture you as you listen to her speak.

INGREDIENTS

8 ounces almond, soy, or flax milk

1 banana, ripe

½ medium avocado or 1 whole small avocado

3 dates

2 tablespoons raw cacao

2 tablespoons almond butter (substitute peanut butter if almond is not convenient)

½ teaspoon ground flaxseed (optional)

Ice as needed

INSTRUCTIONS

1. Combine all ingredients in a blender with approximately ½ cup ice. Process until smooth and serve.

The Sisterhood of the Traveling Pants

ANN BRASHARES

PAIRING: GATORADE, SWEET TEA, PELLEGRINO, OR A SLUSHIE

Take the Sisterhood quiz. Would you be more likely to spend a summer in high school:

> A) At sports camp so you can get an athletic scholarship to a D-1 school;
>
> B) Staying with one of your divorced or separated parents out-of-state;
>
> C) Traveling to a foreign country;
>
> D) Working a job in town to save up money?

If you answered (A) you're BRIDGET! Tall and athletic, you'll want a bottle of Gatorade as you run, swim, and train your way around the Baja California. If you answered (B) you're CARMEN! Spending time in South Carolina with your dad and his new fiancée, you'll be drinking sweet tea all summer as Dad's new family tries to make peace with you before the big wedding. If you answered (C) you're LENA! Traveling with your younger sister Effie to Greece, you'll spend the summer making friends with your Greek grandparents, drinking Pellegrino at cafés, and eating dolmades and Kalamata olives. If you answered (D) you're TIBBY! Hard-working and enterprising, you'll be working hard to save up money for the school year. Tibby spends the first incarnation of the Sisterhood series working at a "Wallmans"—which falls somewhere between a Walgreens and a 7-Eleven. Slurp up an icy, sugary slushie from the convenience store's beverage dispensers and hope the sugar takes the edge off a hard day's work.

The Truth About Forever

SARAH DESSEN

PAIRING: ICED MOCHA

This is a book about trying. Trying to be the perfect daughter. Trying to heal from the sudden death of a parent. Trying to get outside and live a little, even if you don't have a clue what you're doing and need new friends to hold your hand and tug you in the right direction. It's also a book about summer. Summer flings. Summer jobs. Summer SAT prep. What do overworked, underrested teenagers like Macy need when they're trying to survive a desk job with antagonistic librarians, hours of studying vocabulary words, or a crazy night of catering—all in the heat of summer? An ice-cold shot of caffeine. And because most teens don't have dark enough souls yet—or at least they haven't destroyed their taste buds—black coffee isn't going to do the trick. Sweeten your espresso with chocolate syrup and cold milk, pour it all over ice, and you have yourself a little piece of the teenage dream.

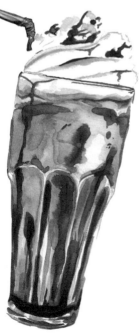

The Hunger Games

SUZANNE COLLINS

PAIRING: BLUEBERRY DAIQUIRI

Love her or hate her, Katniss is an astonishing character. Two of the most dramatic moments in this book center around her willingness to sacrifice herself—first for her sister and then as an act of rebellion against the oppressive ruling class. Self-preservation is not an instinct this girl has in abundance, and yet she's one of the fiercest fighters around. Celebrate her infectious brand of heroism with a drink whose starring ingredient honors her most courageous moment. This blueberry "daiquiri" can be made either nonalcoholic or with rum—and it's a bit more labor-intensive than the rest of the drinks in this book. Rightfully so, because we want to empathize with Katniss and the oppressed, hard-working people from the Districts, not the privileged elites in the Capitol profiting off the labor of others.

INGREDIENTS FOR THE LAVENDER SYRUP
1 tablespoon dried lavender leaves (or 1 bag lavender tea)
1 cup water, a minute or two off the boil
1 cup honey

INSTRUCTIONS
1. Steep lavender leaves in hot water for 2–3 minutes.

2. Remove the tea bag or strain out the tea leaves.

3. Combine honey and lavender tea and stir to mix.

4. Chill on the counter or in the refrigerator to room temperature before using in the drink. (Do not chill below room temperature, as the honey may crystallize.)

INGREDIENTS FOR THE BLUEBERRY SHRUB

1 cup fresh or frozen blueberries
1½ cups apple cider vinegar
2 tablespoons agave nectar or honey

INSTRUCTIONS

1. In a container with a tight-fitting lid, combine blueberries and apple cider vinegar.

2. Shake well and let stand for 2–3 days. Shake once or twice per day to encourage flavor extraction.

3. Strain out blueberries and put shrub in a small saucepan over medium heat. Do not allow to come to a boil.

4. Stir in the agave or honey.

5. Place in a tightly sealed container for storage until ready to use.

INGREDIENTS FOR THE DAIQUIRI

1½ ounces white rum (if using)
¾ ounce lavender syrup
¾ ounce blueberry shrub
Sparkling water
Lavender flowers, for garnish (optional)
Mint sprig, for garnish (optional)
Fresh blueberries, for garnish (optional)

INSTRUCTIONS

1. Combine rum (if using), lavender syrup, and blueberry shrub in a cocktail mixer over ice.

2. Shake well to mix, 10–15 seconds.

3. Fill a highball glass with crushed or small cubes of ice, and drop in a few blueberries, if using.

4. Strain the cocktail into the highball glass.

5. Top with sparkling water, 2–3 ounces or to taste.

6. Garnish with lavender flowers and mint sprig, if using.

(Recipe courtesy of Colleen Graham at The Spruce)

THE VERY THIRSTY CATERPILLAR
KID DRINKS FOR KID LIT

They say smell and taste are the senses most deeply connected to memory creation and access, which is why warm apple cider reminds me of leaf piles and autumn hayrides, and I still can't stand the smell of cooked peas. What better way to share the world's most celebrated children's books with your kids than with a thoughtful drink pairing? By using the pairing as a way to learn about the book, you're giving them a built-in memory tool that will make it easier to remember the lessons within the pages. Your kids will connect with the story more deeply—and you have an excuse to make yourself a drink. Sounds like a win-win to me.

A Visit from St. Nicholas

CLEMENT CLARKE MOORE

PAIRING: Eggnog

"'Twas the night before Christmas when all through the house, not a creature was stirring, not even a mouse." This poem, better known as "The Night Before Christmas," is one of the most famous verses in America and is largely responsible for our idea of Santa Claus and the Christmas Eve ritual of gift-giving. Get in the spirit with eggnog, that fattening, delicious, essential holiday drink. There are so many ways to approach this pairing: dairy companies often produce their own (nonalcoholic) eggnog during the holiday season, which makes it easy to serve for the kids and top it with rum or brandy to taste for the adults. Or you can make your own at home, and build a luxurious cocktail while keeping it virgin for the kids.

INGREDIENTS [YIELDS APPROXIMATELY 1.5 QUARTS]
6 eggs
½ cup + 2 tablespoons sugar
¼ teaspoon salt
4 cups whole milk
1 tablespoon vanilla extract
½ teaspoon ground nutmeg, + more for garnish
1 cup heavy whipping cream
(Optional) Bourbon or dark rum

INSTRUCTIONS
1. Whisk together eggs, sugar, and salt in a large, heavy-bottomed saucepan.

2. Whisk continually while slowly pouring the milk in a steady stream.

3. Set the pan over very low heat and stir continually until the mixture reaches a minimum of 160° F. Be careful not to overheat or boil. This should take between 30–60 minutes depending on your stove.

4. Strain through a fine-mesh sieve into a large bowl to remove any possible bits of cooked egg.

5. Add vanilla and nutmeg, set the mixture in an ice bath, and stir constantly until cool.

6. Cover and refrigerate until cold, up to 3 days before serving.

7. Pour heavy cream into a bowl and whip until it forms soft peaks. Fold the whipped cream into the egg mixture until fully incorporated.

8. Serve in chilled cups and garnish with freshly grated nutmeg.

9. For the adults: top with 1.5–2 ounces rum or bourbon and stir to incorporate.

Alice's Adventures in Wonderland

LEWIS CARROLL

PAIRING: ICED TEA

Would it be right to read this book with anything other than tea? The most famous scene centers around the absurd tea party of the March Hare, the Mad Hatter, and the drowsy Dormouse. Of course, they were most likely drinking hot tea, in the English fashion, but it was a warm summer's day when Alice followed the White Rabbit and went tumbling down the rabbit hole. Between many long walks around Wonderland, violent games of croquet, and a couple adventures in rapidly changing sizes, I'm sure Alice was hot and thirsty—and you will be too, if your kids imitate her adventures. Sip from a sweet and citrusy glass of iced tea as your little ones chase Alice around Wonderland while the poor girl tries to avoid getting her head lopped off.

The Secret Garden
FRANCES HODGSON BURNETT

Pairing: Hibiscus Tea

The intrepid heroine of *The Secret Garden*, "Mistress Mary, quite contrary," demonstrates in this enchanting story of redemption that no one is beyond hope when put in the right circumstances. To make this succulent, inviting tea, hibiscus flowers are blended with various other dried herbs and spices such as orange peel, licorice root, ginger, cinnamon, and even blueberry. You can purchase blends such as Tazo's "Passion" tea (there are many brands, but Tazo is a personal favorite) or you can buy the herbs in bulk and make your own. Whichever you choose, this succulent, floral drink is the perfect evocation of Frances Hodgson Burnett's mysterious, blossoming garden. If you leave the tea bag (or your tea ball) to steep in the glass as you drink, the aromas and flavors will evolve, growing deeper and more concentrated, just like Mary, Colin, and the garden as they awaken from their slumber.

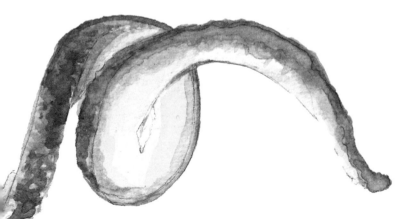

The Story of Ferdinand,
MUNRO LEAF

KIDS' PAIRING: JASMINE TEA
GROWN-UP PAIRING: ALSATIAN GEWÜRZTRAMINER

To join Ferdinand under his cork tree, peacefully smelling the flowers, we want a fragrant, floral drink that takes you to sweet shade on a hot summer's day. For the kids, a warm pot of jasmine tea will do the trick. Jasmine, a member of the olive family whose flowers are as rich and evocative as smells can be, will set the scene perfectly. The same could be said of Gewürztraminer, a pink-skinned grape variety primarily cultivated in Germany, Alsace, and northern Italy. Gewurtztraminer is intensely aromatic and perfumed, evocative of roses, lilac, and tropical fruit. Both drinks will set you right down alongside Ferdinand as he smiles sweetly out over the flowers, be they in ladies' caps or decorating the fields around his idyllic cork tree.

The Little Prince

ANTOINE DE SAINT-EXUPÉRY

PAIRING: SPARKLING WATER

Water is of paramount importance to this tender story. Set primarily in the Sahara where the author's plane has crashed, Saint-Exupéry relates his bittersweet experiences with the visiting prince of a nearby planet. Antoine, an adult, worries about "serious" things, such as the fact that he only has enough water to last him eight days in the desert while he fixes his plane. The young prince, however, has more important things on his mind. From a deadly yellow snake to the fox he tames to the flower on his home planet that has tamed him, the prince explores the world around him with lonely awe. Arguably the most important moment in the story is when the pilot runs out of water and walks into the dunes with his little protégé in search of water. Drink deeply and heartily from this little fount of wisdom, and in the effervescent sparkling water, you may see the little prince's asteroid B-612 twinkling back at you.

Goodnight Moon

MARGARET WISE BROWN AND CLEMENT HURD

PAIRING: HOT COCOA WITH MARSHMALLOWS

A hot fire on a cold night. Two little kittens and a pair of mittens. And a quiet old lady whispering "hush." If you're not drinking hot cocoa with marshmallows with your little ones while reading this essential childhood lullaby, you're doing parenting wrong. (I'm not a parent, so, like men without ovaries who feel inclined to comment on reproductive rights, I clearly have the authority to make this judgment.) If your toddlers have been particularly destructive, I encourage you to add Bailey's to yours. Don't overthink it. This is a simple, elegant pairing for a simple, elegant book.

goodnight

The Lion, the Witch, and the Wardrobe

C. S. LEWIS

PAIRING: ENGLISH BLACK TEA, WITH CREAM AND SUGAR

If you cannot get your hands on "cordial made of the juice of one of the fire-flowers that grow in the mountains of the sun," I suppose a big teapot full of hot tea, served with cream and sugar, is the perfect way to warm up in the chilly land of Narnia in the thrall of the White Witch's spell. (Both fire-flower cordial and hot tea are offered to Peter, Susan, and Lucy by Father Christmas on a cold, snowy night.) This is a great way to introduce the British teatime tradition to your kids, because, let's face it, has there ever been a more British book written for kids in the history of kid's books? (Okay, maybe *Alice's Adventures in Wonderland*.) Drinking piping hot tea with cream and sugar to learn about our cousins across the pond will give your kids a new and exciting way to engage with C. S. Lewis's unforgettable fantasy.

Charlotte's Web

E. B. WHITE

PAIRING: VEGAN MILK

If there was ever a book that could be said to be the standard-bearer for the vegan and vegetarian movement, this is it. Teach your kids where their food comes from and help them be ethical consumers by reading this heartfelt story of a crusader for the condemned life of a farm pig. Explain how pigs and other animals are raised for slaughter, and why Fern and Charlotte had to work so hard to save innocent Wilbur's life. Pair this with a vegan milk that avoids exploitation of dairy cows and explain how America's farming industry systematically exploits animals like Wilbur and his friends to churn out billions of pounds of meat per year. To make it fun instead of serious, set up a taste test with the neighborhood kids and let them pick their favorite vegan milk. There are so many to choose from! From the well-known soy and almond to the increasingly popular hemp, pea, macadamia, and coconut, there are enough nondairy milks on the market to ensure every kid finds a favorite.

The Phantom Tollbooth

NORMAN JUSTER

Pairing: Alphabet soup

With this book-and-drink pairing, you can play with your words *and* your food. (Hey, if you can drink it without a spoon, it's a drink.) Though I recognize we're giving preferential treatment to King Azaz and Dictionopolis, where words rule supreme, at the expense of his brother the Mathematician in Digitopolis, that doesn't mean alphabet soup isn't an excellent pairing for this book of wordplay. While getting lost in the Doldrums, jumping to Conclusions, and searching for the banished sisters of Rhyme and Reason with Tock (oh, how Time Flies!), you can eat your own words as you slurp down some letter-licious alphabet soup.

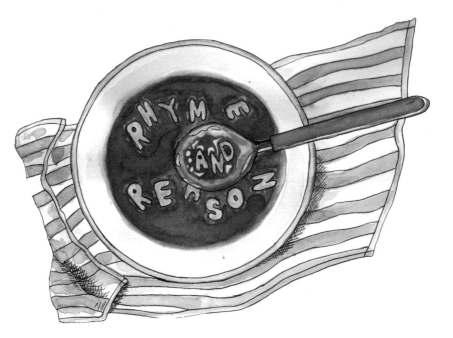

Where the Wild Things Are

MAURICE SENDAK

KIDS' PAIRING: COCA-COLA
GROWN-UP PAIRING: WHISKEY AND COKE

Want to see a magic trick? Your children will spontaneously transform into wild things when you give them each a bottle of Coca-Cola at dinnertime. As any parent knows, caffeine and sugar make a dangerous cocktail in a child's bloodstream. Let the kids run screaming through the house in their monster onesies shooting Nerf guns at each other while you and your partner kick back with a whiskey cola. When they've worn themselves out, it'll be time for a bedtime story, and you can swoop in to the rescue with Maurice Sendak's infamous *Where the Wild Things Are*. "Now stop! Max said, and sent the wild things off to bed." Ask them what's their favorite thing about being a wild thing—and remind them that since they're monsters now, the ones under the bed will be friendly tonight.

Charlie and the Chocolate Factory

ROALD DAHL

PAIRING: CHOCOLATE MILKSHAKE

Did you expect anything else? What better to drink while touring Willy Wonka's famously secretive chocolate factory with his Oompa Loompas than something deliciously chocolatey and gluttonous? Parents can spike theirs with as much bourbon as they deem healthy and kids can paint their faces with chocolate shake as we all dream about finding the Golden Ticket into Willy Wonka's incredible factory. Drink as much as you can now, because once you get inside, you'll want to keep your hands off the goods. We all know what happens when visitors get greedy!

INGREDIENTS (FOR A KID-SIZE SHAKE)
3 scoops chocolate ice cream
¼ cup milk
¼ cup chocolate syrup
1 teaspoon vanilla extract

INSTRUCTIONS
1. Pull the ice cream out of the freezer and let warm until it's the consistency of soft-serve. Chill the milkshake serving glass.

2. Add the ice cream, milk, chocolate syrup, and vanilla extract to a blender.

3. Blend until smooth. Serve in a frosted glass and top with sprinkles. (Bonus points if sourced from Willy Wonka's chocolate factory.)

The Giving Tree

SHEL SILVERSTEIN

PAIRING: APPLE CIDER

Whether you love it or loathe it, the best way to appreciate this book is with a drink that celebrates the tree itself. As kids, we gleefully anticipate autumn, which brings with it the round, earthy sweetness of fresh-squeezed apple juice. As adults, we'll kick back with a crisp bottle of cider just about any time of the year. Whether the cider is fermented or not, when you and your kids are sipping from a cool glass full of the kind apple tree's fruits, you'll find yourself grateful for the spirit of generosity reflected in Silverstein's controversial parable.

The Very Hungry Caterpillar
ERIC CARLE

PAIRING: FRUIT CORDIAL

Take your kids on a sip-able journey as they follow the hungry caterpillar stocking up on calories before his transformation into a butterfly. A fruit cordial, with apple, pear, and strawberry, will let the kids mirror the caterpillar's foodie adventures while you read together. Be sure to read this one in the morning—or else water it back with lots of seltzer—lest the rush of sugar inspire the kids to eat their way through everything in the house before bedtime.

INGREDIENTS (MAKES APPROXIMATELY 2 PINTS CORDIAL, OR 4 FINISHED SERVINGS)
1 pound cored, washed apples, sliced and cut into thin, 1-inch pieces
1 pound cored, washed pears, sliced and cut into thin, 1-inch pieces
1 pound fresh strawberries, washed and sliced, plus extra for garnish.
¼ cup fresh lemon juice
9 cups water
2¼ cups sugar
2 pints soda water, for serving

INSTRUCTIONS
1. Combine apples, pears, and strawberries in a large mixing bowl. Pour the lemon juice over the top and toss or stir to coat.

2. Bring the water to a boil. When it is boiling, stir in the sugar until it is dissolved. Remove from heat.

3. Pour over the fruit and let rest until room temperature.

4. Cover and refrigerate for 12–24 hours.

5. Strain through a fine mesh sieve to separate cordial from fruit. (Save the leftover fruit for ice cream or pie toppings.)

6. To serve, mix 1 part cordial with 1 part soda water, or to taste. Top with ice and garnish with fresh, sliced strawberries.

The Lorax

DR. SEUSS

Pairing: Rooibos Tea

The rooibos plant, grown exclusively in the Western Cape of South Africa, produces an earthy tea reminiscent of wood and autumn leaves and is warm and earthy in flavor. Rooibos is more of a bush than a tree, but if you imagine this grassy, green-and-yellow plant at the end of a lanky trunk, it could pass for a truffula tree. Which is fitting, since both truffula and rooibos are threatened by the rising tides of man-made (or Once-Ler-made) climate change. As the Western Cape heats up in the summer and the winters become drier, the rooibos plant will eventually be unable to survive. Scientists predict rooibos could be extinct within a century, making rooibos tea the perfect thing to serve your little ones while you read Dr. Seuss's prescient book heralding the dangers of environmental destruction at the hands of industry. Explain to them that, "Unless someone like you cares a whole awful lot," rooibos, like the truffula, will disappear. "It's not going to get better—it's not."

If You Give a Mouse a Cookie

LAURA JOFFE NUMEROFF

PAIRING: MILK (OR PLANT-BASED MILK)

If you give a kid a bedtime story, he's going to ask for something to drink. This pairing is obvious by the time you turn to the first page. Pour the kids a big glass of milk, warm or cold, as you read this story to them at night. The kids probably won't notice how similar the mouse's adorable but unending demands are to their own—that's a blissful lack of self-awareness that only comes with youth—but that shouldn't stop you from enjoying this charming book of kid-size logic.

The Golden Compass

PHILIP PULLMAN

KID'S PAIRING: GINGER BEER
GROWN-UP PAIRING: GINGER-BOURBON JULEP

The Golden Compass was my favorite book growing up. Lyra Silvertongue (née Belacqua) was the fierce ruffian I needed to guide me into adolescence as a tomboyish, independent teenager. I idolized her. It's no surprise, then, that the pairing also happens to be one of my favorite drinks. Ginger beer—blond, spirited, and daring—could not more perfectly capture Lyra's essence. And a Ginger-Bourbon Julep—kind of a mash-up of a Moscow Mule and a Mint Julep—is the perfect way to bring youthful flavors into an adult drink. When I think back to our neighborhood kids' book club, I imagine both kids and parents would have loved to have something like this near at hand as we talked about this book. Garnish your kids' cups with a few sprigs of mint so theirs are as pretty as yours, and as you read (and drink), talk to them about all the characteristics that make Lyra such an inspiring heroine.

INGREDIENTS (FOR THE GINGER-BOURBON JULEP)
Fresh mint leaves (at least 8–10 per cup, preferably more), plus more for garnish
1 teaspoon sugar
3 ounces bourbon
4–5 ounces ginger beer

INSTRUCTIONS
1. In a cocktail shaker, muddle together mint and sugar for 10–15 seconds or until sugar is starting to dissolve.

2. Top with bourbon, fill glass with ice, and shake well.

3. Strain into a cocktail glass, and top with ice and ginger beer.

4. Garnish with mint sprigs and serve.

The Bad Beginning

LEMONY SNICKET

KID'S PAIRING: LEMONADE
GROWN-UP PAIRING: LEMONADE AND VODKA

The phrase "when life gives you lemons, make lemonade,"—an expression that here means "when bad things happen in life, you have to make the best of it"—is perhaps best represented in fiction by Violet, Klaus, and Sunny Baudelaire. (Any resemblance of the word "lemonade" to the author's first name is purely coincidental.) Enterprising and determined in the face of dire, often abusive situations, the Baudelaire siblings manage to remain as sweet as lemonade to those around them but as sharp as a zingy slice of lemon. Between Violet's inventions, Klaus's book knowledge, and Sunny's sharp teeth, the siblings use their wits and weapons to keep evil at bay—and their chins up as they do.

INGREDIENTS
6–7 fresh lemons
1 cup simple syrup
2–3 cups cold water

INSTRUCTIONS
1. Juice all but one of the lemons. You should have between 1 and 1½ cups of juice, depending on the size of the lemons.

2. Combine 1 cup lemon juice (reserving remainder) and simple syrup in a pitcher.

3. Dilute to taste with 2–3 cups of water and stir. (Remember that ice will dilute the lemonade further, so it's best to make it just a little stronger than you'd like at this stage.) If the mixture is too sweet, add reserved lemon juice.

4. Fill pitcher with ice. Fill serving glasses with ice and pour lemonade into glasses. Garnish with a slice of lemon per glass.

The Book Thief

MARKUS ZUSAK

PAIRING: ORANGE FANTA

Fanta, the orange soda beloved the world over, didn't remotely resemble its current form until the 1950s. Invented during the World War II era in Germany as a replacement for Coca-Cola, Fanta gets a bad rap as having been invented "for" or "by" the Nazi regime. It wasn't. (That doesn't mean you can't still give it some suspicious side-eye, but we should do that with *all* sodas, not just Fanta.) When Hitler's armies invaded Europe and war broke out, the Coca-Cola company stopped supplying their German factories with the syrups needed to make the drink. Max Keith, the leader of the German wing of Coca-Cola's operations and an enterprising businessman, decided to make his own. Fanta, whose name derives from the German word *fantasie*, was born. Then, Fanta was a pale, fizzy soda reminiscent of ginger ale. And although the Fanta of today might not resemble the Fanta of Liesel Meminger's day, the brand would have been one of the only sodas available to families like hers. Get up close and personal with Death, Zusak's unforgettable narrator, as you read this devastating novel of love, loss, and the power of storytelling.

ACKNOWLEDGMENTS

There were so many people who helped bring this book to life, whether by encouragement, advice, consultation, or simply sharing their joy and delight when I explained the idea of pairing great drinks with great books. It would be impossible to name everyone, so I wish to begin by thanking all those of you who have ever dropped me a word of encouragement, helped me when I was stuck, offered opinions on the books and the pairings herein, or expressed their enthusiasm for books and drinks more generally. I also wish to thank those of you who discovered my writing through the *Seeds* trilogy. Without your support of those books, I might never have dared to call myself a writer.

There are a number of people who deserve particular thanks, though the debt of gratitude I owe them ensures these little words cannot do them justice.

First, to my mother Kristy, a publisher and writer whose dream provided the genesis for my writing career when we began to write *The Sowing* together with Elena. You are unfailingly supportive, encouraging, and talented, and without your advice and vision I might not have started writing in the first place, and this book would never have been born.

Next, to my breathtakingly talented sister Elena, who provided the gorgeous mixed-media illustrations that grace the cover and interior of this book. Everything you do astounds and inspires me, and I am eternally grateful to you for volunteering to take on this project even during your first chaotic year of art school. Despite the madness of your schedule, the illustrations you've provided for this book are everything I hoped for and so much more.

To Andrea Somberg, who spotted a naïve but determined writer in a massive slush pile and called that writer not two days later, thereby massively reducing my stress and workload by ensuring I would only ever have to send one query about this book. Thank you for believing in me and in the books-and-booze concept, and for all the work you have done and continue to do to help make *Literary Libations* a reality.

To the other half of that equation, Leah Zarra and the Skyhorse team: thank you for taking on this book, for your faith in this project, for your kind words of encouragement, and for carefully cleaning up my haphazard, disorganized cocktail recipes.

There are a few people who provided consultation throughout the process or advice on a particular drink, and they deserve commendation by name as well: Prashant Parmar, wizard and medic extraordinaire, who consulted on a number of the fantasy and science fiction titles in this book and gave me advice about which to read; Kateland Carr, who introduced me to the Muscadine wine that accompanies *To Kill a Mockingbird*; Bernard Pilon and Daryl Rothman, both of whom have endlessly encouraged me in my writing pursuits and both of whom I count as mentors and advisors on my literary, artistic, and culinary career; Stasha Migliaccio and Eva Ford, both avid readers whose encouragement, wisdom, and literary experience I depended on as I selected the books to be included in *Literary Libations*; and Sky Evans, whose guiding philosophy of self-awareness has helped steer me through stress, anxiety, and fear over the last few years, and whose wild and artistic spirit never fails to inspire.

Of all my consultants, advice-givers, and providers of support, the one to whom I owe the deepest debt of gratitude is Vincent Vidrine. As a winemaker, beer drinker, cocktail aficionado, avid home cook, dance partner, and life copilot, you were the impetus and inspiration behind a dozen or more of the drinks in this book—from the Calvados that accompanies *Madam Bovary* to the Boilermaker for *The Shining* and so many more—and always knew just when I was most in need of a pep talk. I cannot thank you enough for the support and love you've shown since the moment I met you. I love you. Thank you.

Last, but by no means least, to my father and fellow author Jason Makansi, who called me up the day after I wrote an off-the-cuff blog post about pairing literary genres with different types of wine and said it was very funny and had I considered turning it into a book? Without you, *What to Drink with What You Read* would never have been more than a blog post in an obscure corner of the Internet. Thank you for being you, and for inspiring me to dream big.

CONVERSION CHARTS
METRIC AND IMPERIAL CONVERSIONS

(These conversions are rounded for convenience)

Ingredient	Cups/ Tablespoons/ Teaspoons	Ounces	Grams/ Milliliters
Fruit, dried	1 cup	4 ounces	120 grams
Fruits or veggies, chopped	1 cup	5 to 7 ounces	145 to 200 grams
Fruits or veggies, puréed	1 cup	8.5 ounces	245 grams
Honey, maple syrup, or corn syrup	1 tablespoon	0.75 ounce	20 grams
Liquids: cream, milk, water, or juice	1 cup	8 fluid ounces	240 milliliters
Salt	1 teaspoon	0.2 ounces	6 grams
Spices: cinnamon, cloves, ginger, or nutmeg (ground)	1 teaspoon	0.2 ounce	5 milliliters
Sugar, brown, firmly packed	1 cup	7 ounces	200 grams
Sugar, white	1 cup/ 1 tablespoon	7 ounces/0.5 ounce	200 grams/12.5 grams
Vanilla extract	1 teaspoon	0.2 ounce	4 grams

LIQUIDS

8 fluid ounces = 1 cup = ½ pint
16 fluid ounces = 2 cups = 1 pint
32 fluid ounces = 4 cups = 1 quart
128 fluid ounces = 16 cups = 1 gallon

INDEX